DEBRA OSWALD is a writer for stage, film, television, radio and children's fiction.

Debra's plays have been produced by theatre companies around Australia, including Playbox, Griffin, State Theatre of South Australia, the Ensemble and the Q Theatre. *Gary's House* and *Sweet Road* were both shortlisted for the NSW Premier's Award. Her play *Dags* has had many Australian productions and has been published and performed in Britain and the United States. *Gary's House* is on the senior high school syllabus in NSW and has been performed in Denmark in translation. The Australian Theatre for Young People commissioned Debra to write *Skate*, which had a Sydney season and a NSW country tour in 2003. *Skate* will tour to the Belfast Theatre Festival in October 2005.

Mr Bailey's Minder won the 2003 Griffin Award for a new play and in 2004 was produced by Griffin Theatre (Sydney) and Riverina Theatre Company. The season was a box office record for Griffin and that production will tour extensively in NSW, Victoria, Queensland and the Northern Territory in 2006.

Debra television writing credits including *Bananas in Pyjamas*, *Palace of Dreams*, *Sweet and Sour*, *The Secret Life of Us* and award-winning episodes of *Police Rescue*. One of her *Police Rescue* episodes, 'Wildcard', won a silver medal at the New York Festivals.

Debra is also author of seven children's novels, published by Penguin in Australia, which have been variously published in France, Italy, Norway, Sweden and Germany. Her children's books include *The Redback Leftovers*, *The Fifth Quest* and *Frank and the Secret Club*.

Kate Mulvany as Therese in the 2004 Griffin Theatre production.
(Photo: Robert McFarlane)

Mr Bailey's Minder

Debra Oswald

Currency Press, Sydney

CURRENCY PLAYS

First published in 2005
by Currency Press Pty Ltd,
PO Box 2287, Strawberry Hills, NSW, 2012, Australia
enquiries@currency.com.au
www.currency.com.au

NATIONAL LIBRARY OF AUSTRALIA CIP DATA
    Oswald, Debra.
        Mr Bailey's minder.
        ISBN 0 86819 761 0.
        I. Title.
        (Series: Currency plays).
    A822.3

Publication of this title was assisted by
the Commonwealth Government through
the Australia Council, its arts funding
and advisory body.

Set by Dean Nottle
Cover design by Kate Florance, Currency Press
Front cover shows Kate Mulvany as Therese and Martin Vaughan as Leo in the
2004 Griffin Theatre production. (Photo: Robert McFarlane).

Contents

Currency Press acknowledges the Traditional Owners of the Country on which
we live and work. We pay our respects to all Aboriginal and Torres Strait
Islander Elders, past and present.

Introduction

Christopher Hurrell

'*It's like Leo can see the specialness inside a thing so when a person looks at the painting they can see it too.*'

'*Leo Bailey is like a sac of poison in my belly. Toxins leak out into my system if I'm not vigilant.*'

How can the two men described above be one and the same? This is the conundrum that haunts *Mr Bailey's Minder*. The history of art is full of anecdotes about tortured artists destroying their own lives and those of others; tormenting their family and friends with temper, capriciousness and cruelty. In short, stories of great artists failing to be even mediocre human beings.

How do we reconcile this with the fact that the artist's gift is the ability to 'see the specialness inside a thing'—a talent that would seem to be synonymous with the 'emotional imagination' necessary for compassion?

Leo Bailey is Australia's greatest living artist. However, *Mr Bailey's Minder* is not a play about the nature of art, or of artists, though observations on those two subjects feed into the play's heart. It is a play richly infused with the remarkable spirit of its author: compassionate, insightful and ethical. Debra's ethic is both demanding and forgiving. On the one hand, the play seems to say there is no excuse for behaviour that damages those who share the earth with us. On the other hand, it reassures us: if we find this challenge difficult to meet, we should take heart because even those blessed with a genius for seeing and understanding others often find it almost impossible.

The theme of healing damaged souls is a recurring one in Debra's work and it is one which is central to *Mr Bailey's Minder*. It is an essential element to the theatrical experience she creates. The ultimate ambition of a play such as *Mr Bailey's Minder* goes beyond telling a story of souls healing together. Through the power, human complexity and catharsis of that story, it creates an experience that is spiritually restorative for its audience. Critics often struggle to define the experience of a Debra Oswald play. Perhaps the most apt, simple description of her work came from the *Age*'s Helen Thomson, who described it as containing 'authentic optimism'. Debra constructs dramatic situations loaded with genuine, complex human suffering and shortcoming, and then finds credible, difficult resolution. It seems to offer us real hope that even the darkest passages of our lives can be successfully navigated; that it's never too late to find healing. You may be stuck with the scars, and things will never be perfect, but rehabilitation is possible and worth seeking.

Therese struggles with self-loathing. She brings into Leo Bailey's house resilience, an experience of deprivation and, above all things, ignorance. She has no idea who Leo Bailey is. The fact that he's famous and talented means nothing to her. Thus from the outset, Leo is unable to find the weak-spot in her that he has found in perhaps every other person he's met in at least a quarter of a century.

It doesn't take him long to locate a weakness in Therese, but it comes with a surprise: an aggressive, instinctive defence mechanism. No one is going to inflame the wounds of her self-doubt without a sharp jab in return.

Therese, unlike Leo, has a lifetime's experience of true deprivation: imprisonment, betrayal, failure. Yet she possesses a resilience and strength that leaves Leo for dead. She responds to her extensive, tangible suffering with determination to do better. Her example reveals that the 'artist's tortured inner life' justification is a childish indulgence.

Leo's experience of deprivation is much more recent and unfamiliar to him. He's outraged to find, through age and deterioration, that he is no longer at unbridled liberty to do as he pleases. 'I wanted to go out. Out', he squawks petulantly, early in the play. Faced with someone infinitely stronger than himself, he is nonplussed. He begins to capitulate. The strange combination of real care with steadfast refusal to indulge him is the first decent medicine offered him after years of physical and mental sickness.

And so the healing begins. Therese eloquently describes the feeling of debilitating shame and Leo regains a little of the self-awareness that deserted him years ago in a storm of sycophancy, alcohol abuse, creative frenzy and self-obsession.

THERESE: Some memory oozes up and eats away at your guts, eh. You know what I think about sometimes? When I'm in the shower, I tip my head back and I let the water run down my face and neck and I imagine if the water could wash it all away…

LEO: The shame.

THERESE: Yeah. Wash away every bad thing I ever did. Start again, clean.

Two more damaged souls inhabit the play. Leo's daughter Margo is a complex figure, who surprisingly turns out to be the play's emotional centre. She is responsible for managing Leo's life, and she does so with cool detachment. It's she who hires Therese to care for him. Margo is also responsible for sending the tradesman Karl into the house, to remove one of the few remaining art works of value. Like Margo, but for totally different reasons, Karl is one of life's 'stayers'. Their own wounds have left them suffering from opposite deficiencies. Margo is no longer able to see the good in others, Karl no longer able to see the bad. But it's the staying quality in both these characters, as well as in Therese, that holds these four people together to redeem each other.

The silent character in this play is the house. Leo doesn't live in a real house—rather a shack pulled together from his life and art. The house, and the remnants of the art it contains, also play their part in the healing. Therese's early success with Leo leads them out of the tumbledown prison and, by chance, into one of the temples of capitalism in the city centre, where Therese for the first time comes face-to-face with one of Leo's great works adorning an imposing corporate foyer:

THERESE: It's like there's a light inside the painting shining directly on me, filling me up, sending an electric charge through my blood into every tiny cell of me.

The play binds belief in the redemptive power of art into its human core, but refuses to mythologise it or its creators. It tells us that talents and abilities—of any kind—are immaterial. The difficult responsibility of caring for fellow-souls is one we all must struggle with in order to honour our own humanity.

◆ ◆ ◆ ◆ ◆

As director of the first production of a new play, one of the first challenges I face is to establish its performance style. It is customary to think of Debra purely as a practitioner of Australian Naturalism. This, however, is inaccurate and misses the point of Debra's work. While her plays are largely naturalistic in form, the sensibility that governs them is innately theatrical. Debra herself is the first to proclaim 'I'm not a stylist', but it is instructive that one of her theatrical heroes when she began writing plays as a teenager was Joe Orton, with his heightened, radical, subversive comedies.

Debra's work exists as much in a tradition of wild theatrical comedy as any other. The sensibility comes from, say, Molière, bequeathed to her via Orton and, more locally, the knockabout comedy of the Australian New-Wave, which she experienced first-hand as part of Nimrod's earliest audiences at Sydney's tiny Stables Theatre, more than thirty years before this play would premiere in the same theatre. She describes sitting in the front row as a child, entranced by Reg Livermore, as the experience which called her to the theatre. It was to Molière that I first looked when developing the performance style with which to bring *Mr Bailey's Minder* to the stage. It might be difficult to recognise the complex characters described above as archetypes—but they jump off the page as being such, and with good reason. The archetype is a crucial ingredient of such comedy, developed as it was from the Commedia del'Arte. Debra's work synthesises these techniques seamlessly with the complex character flaws and journeys found in Chekhov, to deliver, perhaps paradoxically, an intrinsically Australian theatrical world, inhabited by warmth and roughness, empathy and absurdity, broad humour and searing pathos.

The first production of *Mr Bailey's Minder* contained many exquisite moments of humour and humanity conjured on stage by Martin Vaughan, Kate Mulvany, Victoria Longley and Andy Rodoreda. Those moments lie in, around and underneath the words you are about to read. And so I urge you to read slowly, intuitively and with an open heart.

Christopher Hurrell directed Griffin Theatre's
premiere production at Sydney's Stable Theatre.

Debra Oswald would like to thank Christopher Hurrell, Michael Wynne, Richard Glover, Karen Oswald, Gillian Higginson, Kerry Laurence, Amanda Higgs, David Middlebrook, David Berthold, Griffin Theatre, Riverina Theatre Company, Currency Press, the cast and creative team of the 2004 production.

For Nick Nickleby, with much love

Mr Bailey's Minder was first produced by Griffin Theatre Company in association with Riverina Theatre Company at the SBW Stables Theatre, Kings Cross, Sydney, on 29 July 2004 with the following cast:

MARGO	Victoria Longley
THERESE	Kate Mulvany
GAVIN / KARL	Andy Rodoreda
LEO BAILEY	Martin Vaughan

Director, Christopher Hurrell
Designer, Jo Briscoe
Lighting Designer, Stephen Hawker
Music and Sound Designer, Basil Hogios

CHARACTERS

THERESE, mid-20s
MARGO, late 30s
LEO BAILEY, late 60s
GAVIN, 30s
KARL, about 30

The play is written for four performers.
The roles of Gavin and Karl should be played by the same actor.

SETTING

Leo Bailey's house.

ACT ONE

SCENE ONE

Leo Bailey's house is a fabulous, precarious, ramshackle, brightly-coloured construction.

It's built into the cliff with part of a wall and floor chiselled out of the rock face. The rest of the structure is made up of unlikely materials tacked together—old ferry doors, church windows, car bonnets, packing crates. Most surfaces are spattered with thick gobs of paint. There are many adapted and bowerbirded items, including New Guinea artefacts. A narrow, wonky staircase leads to the upper floor.

There are a couple of large paintings that have had paint thrown all over them, obliterating the original image.

There are empty bottles and plates with half-rotten food strewn around the house.

MARGO *ushers* THERESE *in from the front door.* MARGO *is in her late thirties, wearing expensive business clothes.*

MARGO: Watch your step. Foot's just as likely to go straight through a rotten board.

> THERESE *is in her mid-twenties, a bit of a scrag, boisterous, defensive, volatile. She carries two cheap sportsbags.*

Did the employment agency explain what the job is?

THERESE: Yeah. Well, y'know, they said—

MARGO: I don't want to waste my time and yours if you're not serious.

THERESE: Oh no, no, I'm serious. I mean, I want the job, if you want me.

MARGO: You realise you would have to live here full-time?

THERESE: Yep. Yep. Is that the door off a ferry?

MARGO: There've been magazine articles about the house if you're interested. You would have to live here as is. My father won't have anything changed.

THERESE: Yeah. Whatever.

MARGO: Water runs down the wall when it rains.

THERESE: Is that real rock or fake rock?

MARGO: That wall is the cliff-face.

THERESE: Yeah? It's up so high, eh. View's incredible. The harbour and all those rich dickheads' boats tied up out there—

> THERESE *rouses on herself under her breath, wanting to control her mouth.*

MARGO: Have you got a resume? References?

THERESE: Oh, yeah.

> MARGO *flicks through the papers* THERESE *hands her.*

I'm not a nurse or anything so if you need like an actual nurse, I'm not.

MARGO: My father can't stand having a nurse in the house. But he needs a live-in carer. We tried having people come in on a daily basis but he was up half the night setting fire to things.

THERESE: Is he mental? Oh—s'pose it sounds rude, asking straight out like that.

MARGO: You need to know if you'll be the one cleaning up the vomit.

THERESE: Cleaned up bucketloads of vomit in my time.

> *She laughs.* MARGO *looks at her.*

Oh—I mean—I've had a few friends who—well, not so much friends as— I'm just saying I'm not fazed by stuff like vomit.

> THERESE *curses herself for losing control of her mouth.*

MARGO: Leo has alcohol-related dementia. Aggravated by various subdural haematomas from falling down various sets of stairs when drunk. Also chronic obstructive airways disease, chronic alcoholic hepatitis, cirrhosis of the liver and ulcers. He's a wet-brain.

THERESE: Okay… so is he out somewhere right now?

MARGO: He doesn't leave the house anymore. Except for visits to medical specialists. [*She bellows towards the stairs.*] Leo! Come out! Come and meet—!

> *She looks at the references.*

THERESE: Therese.

MARGO: Therese!

No response.

He's hiding.

THERESE *glances nervously at the papers in* MARGO's *hands.*

THERESE: Look, if you wanna know how come I left the last job, the guy was a total arsehole. Some mongrels'll never give you a decent go. The guy had it in for me—

MARGO: I'm really not interested—

LEO: [*yelling down the stairs*] Get out! Get out of my house!

THERESE: Oh—uh—should I—?

MARGO: He's talking to me, not you.

LEO: I can hear you! I can hear you down there, you lying bitch!

MARGO: [*to* THERESE] It's me.

THERESE *looks at pictures up high on the wall.*

THERESE: He's a famous artist, right? He did those paintings?

MARGO: Well, they're the remains of murals. He threw tins of house paint on the parts lower down. Up there, he couldn't reach.

THERESE: Does he do it anymore?

MARGO: He stopped several years ago. Even back then, he was only doing the odd scribble when he needed cash.

THERESE *screws up her face at the pictures, embarrassed.*

THERESE: I don't know what's supposed to be good or—

MARGO: The man you'd be looking after is a drunk, not an artist. You don't need to know anything for this job.

THERESE: [*indicating the resume*] Are you gonna ring the employers on there?

MARGO: Well, I don't know if I'll ring any—

THERESE: You've gotta ring them. I know that's how it works. But if you ring that second guy, don't believe a word that comes out of his poxy, lying mouth. He'll badmouth me and— But hey—not one person'd tell you I ever bashed up old guys or anything like that. Fuck. Switch off your mouth, Therese.

MARGO: I don't think you're going to have—

THERESE: You don't think I'm right for the job. Big surprise. Why did you bother getting me to come down here, if you were never gonna—? Ohhh… I better just go.

THERESE *grabs her bags.*

MARGO: Look, Ms Laurence—

THERESE: Hey. I wasn't asking anyone to do me any favours.

MARGO: I wasn't planning to do you any favours.

THERESE: Yeah, der. People like you always reckon— Oh, bugger it, I'll get out of your way. [*She starts to leave again.*] I'd appreciate it if you didn't say anything to the job people about me stuffing this up.

MARGO: Well, I was actually hoping to—

THERESE: Yeah? It's your business. I can't stop you. I was asking you to give me a break but if you want to be a total bitch about it then fuck it. [*She turns to go but then spins back.*] I dunno why you think you can look down your nose at me. I mean, you're the one who wants to pay a total stranger to look after your dad. Jesus.

There are hissing noises from the stairs.

LEO: Viper!

THERESE *jumps in fright but* MARGO *is matter-of-fact.*

MARGO: If you want to meet Therese, you'd better hurry. She says she's leaving.

LEO *comes down the stairs. He is in his late sixties, rheumy-eyed, with a face battered and bloated by years of boozing. He's wearing grubby pyjamas.*

LEO: [*to* THERESE] Step away from her. Very slowly and calmly. They can smell fear.

THERESE: Sorry?

LEO: Viper! She's a viper! Step away from her!

MARGO: This is Leo Bailey.

THERESE: Hi. I'm Therese.

LEO *circles* MARGO, *making snake hissing noises.* MARGO *ignores him and goes through papers in her briefcase.*

LEO: Did The Viper tell you she works in investment banking? Investment banking! The dead hand. Feast your eyes! She's a dried-up bitch. Have you asked her why she's got no children?

THERESE: Uh…

LEO: Because she's a dried-up bitch—I just told you! She had one grotesque marriage to a shrivelled-up loser of a bloke and she couldn't even hang onto him. Ask her why.

THERESE: None of my business, really.

LEO *grabs Therese's bags and thrusts them into her hands.*

LEO: Hang onto your purse. Soon as you look away, she's pinching stuff. Oh yes, oh yes. Ask The Viper where she's hiding all my paintings she stole!

MARGO: Ask me.

THERESE: Oh, right. Where are all the paintings you stole?

MARGO: I've never stolen any paintings.

THERESE: Right.

Victoria Longley as Margo in the 2004 Griffin Theatre production. (Photo: Robert McFarlane)

LEO *crumbles into incoherent muttering, retreating to a corner.* MARGO *hands* THERESE *back her resume.*

MARGO: Okay then.

THERESE: I'll bugger off and you can interview the other desperates.

MARGO: The other desperates weren't interested. I meant 'Okay then, the job's yours'.

THERESE: Oh.

MARGO *sees* THERESE's *stunned mullet expression.*

MARGO: Do you want the job? If anything's changed your mind, tell me now before—

THERESE: Uh—yeah. I mean, no I haven't changed my mind. Y'know— Yes, I want the job.

MARGO: I'm due at an appointment so I can't go through everything with you now. Do you need time to move out from where you are?

THERESE: No. No. Ready to roll.

MARGO: You don't need to collect the rest of your luggage?

THERESE: No. This is it.

MARGO *glances at Therese's two pathetic bags then gets a folder of papers out of her briefcase.*

MARGO: Information about doctors' appointments and medications. Bills are paid through my office. An agency nurse will come Sundays nine to four to give you a day off. It's a different one every time so do your best to fill them in. Anyway, it's all in there. [*Her mobile phone rings and she looks at the display.*] Look, any questions you really can't sort out on your own, leave a message with my assistant. Okay?

THERESE: Okay. And, y'know, don't worry or anything. I can work things out.

MARGO: I'm sure.

THERESE: And thanks for—y'know—

MARGO *jerks an awkward smile and leaves, answering her mobile phone.* THERESE *takes a deep breath.* LEO *peers at her from his corner.* THERESE *starts tidying up the room.*

LEO: You're an art student.

THERESE: No.

LEO: They tried that. Getting art students in here. 'Ooh, Mr Bailey, you're so brilliant.' Nauseating.

THERESE: I'm not an art student.

LEO: Overseas student. Backpacker. You don't sound foreign.

THERESE: Not unless you count Cessnock as foreign.

LEO: Aaahhh… you're a penniless writer.

THERESE: No.

LEO: I know. I know. You're a—

THERESE: I'm Therese. I'm not anything.

> LEO *snatches a plate of half-eaten food from* THERESE's *hand.*

LEO: Oy, I'm still eating that.

THERESE: Give us a break. There's hairy stuff growing on it.

> LEO *grumbles but lets her take it.*

LEO: You look nothing like my third wife. She was a flame-haired goddess.

THERESE: Third wife?

LEO: I married five of the most beautiful women in Australia.

THERESE: Five?

LEO: Women who could have had any man they wanted. They picked me. I don't find you attractive at all.

THERESE: Yeah? Bingo. I don't find you attractive either. So that's lucky, eh?

LEO: What? What are you squawking about? You've got an ugly voice. Ugly.

THERESE: It's lucky because this arrangement wouldn't work if we were hot for each other.

LEO: My wife was a hot woman. Like sleeping next to an open fire.

THERESE: Maybe it was something to do with being a flame-haired goddess.

LEO: Not that wife! The one before! Are you stupid stupid stupid?

THERESE: Hey. Don't give me shit, Leo. Are you this nasty to everyone? Not surprised you're on your own.

LEO *grabs paint and a brush. He daubs a family tree on a wall or window pane.*

LEO: How many times do I have to go through this? First I married Phyllis. Children: Margo. Second wife—

THERESE: Margo who was here before?

LEO: The Viper, yes. [*Painting odd letters and symbols*] Second wife: Patricia. Three children: Henry, Greta, Roland. Wife number three—

THERESE: The flame-haired goddess.

LEO: Yes. Now we're getting somewhere. No children with her. Or with Maria—couldn't get it up by then.

THERESE: So you've got four kids?

LEO: No. More. Eight that I know of.

THERESE: Four kids still unaccounted for.

LEO: I'm hungry. That's why I can't think. I missed out a wife.

LEO *peers at the family tree, grunting with frustration.*

THERESE: Leave a gap and you can fill them in later, eh.

LEO: They're all monsters, anyway. All my children turned out to be monsters.

THERESE: I'll scrounge us some lunch.

THERESE *rummages around in the mess of the kitchen area.*

LEO: I'm Australia's greatest living artist!

THERESE: What was that, mate?

LEO: I'm a national living treasure!

THERESE: Yeah? Bit of boaster, aren'cha Leo?

LEO: I never had one painting lesson. My father—this is in New Guinea— my father thought painting was only for bored ex-pat wives.

THERESE: You grew up in New Guinea?

LEO: Shoosh! I'm talking. My father laughed at my paintings. I had to paint on bits of old masonite. Now they're worth thousands of bloody dollars!

THERESE: Woo-hoo! There's a tin of sardines.

LEO: Shut up! Don't talk about sardines when I'm trying to tell you something.

THERESE: Fancy sardines for lunch?

LEO: I'm explaining something and you keep talking about sardines!

THERESE: I don't keep talking about sardines. I only said the word twice. Well, now I've said it three times but only because you—

LEO: Who are you? Why would anyone want this job? You must be a loser, a no-hoper. I can see why. Look at you. A grubby, ignorant, gauche nobody.

> THERESE *fixes him with a fierce look.*

THERESE: You know what, Leo? If you wanna have a slagging match with me, I reckon I'd wipe the floor with you. So I wouldn't recommend trying it, all right? If you wanna ring your daughter and get me sacked right now, then fuck you.

> LEO *shrinks away from* THERESE, *afraid of her.*

LEO: Did she do the list of things that are wrong with me?

THERESE: Yes. I'm going to have a proper study of the doctors' notes later.

LEO: I'm going to die.

THERESE: Nah—I won't let that happen. If you die, I'm out of a job and homeless.

> *She can see that* LEO *is very panicky.*

Are you feeling crook right now? Probably hungry mostly. I'll—

LEO: Every day more bits of my body start rotting. I can feel my lungs crumbling away like a perished sponge. I'm not even dead yet and the rotting's started.

THERESE: Well, it's my job to keep you alive.

> LEO *grabs her hand like a lifeline.* THERESE *is startled but lets him hang on.*

LEO: Can you stop my body falling apart? No. You can't.

THERESE: Hey. Hey. Leo. Don't panic, mate.

> LEO *whimpers, clinging to* THERESE*'s hand.*

It's okay, Leo. You're not dying right now, I don't reckon.

> LEO *pulls away from her and shuffles out.*

SCENE TWO

LEO, *wearing pyjama pants and a dirty singlet, stumbles around the room looking for something.*

THERESE *shouts from the top of the stairs, carrying a towel, clean clothes and a pair of shoes.*

THERESE: You little dickhead—get in that bathroom and have a shower!

LEO: Where is it?

THERESE: If you're looking for the scotch, it's upstairs.

LEO: Go and get it.

THERESE: No way. Get it yourself if you want more.

LEO: Mean-spirited bitch.

THERESE: Let's get you washed. You stink.

LEO: Keep your hands off me. No shower. I don't want to get wet.

THERESE: Put on clean clothes at least. Let's get that festy singlet off you.

LEO: You know nothing! I've had books written about me. Thousands of words!

> THERESE *tries to get his singlet off him.* LEO *fights her off, whacking* THERESE *in the eye. She hisses with pain and yanks him round by the shoulder.*

THERESE: That's enough.

LEO: Are you going to hit me?

> THERESE *realises she's got her hand raised, about to hit him. She drops her hand.*

THERESE: No. You shut up now and let me—

LEO: Your fingers are hurting me. Digging into my skin.

> THERESE *drops away the hand that's holding his shoulder.*

THERESE: Stink all fucking day if you want.

> LEO *makes a big show of putting on the shoes.*

How can you be this drunk this early in the day? Atchally, don't answer that.

LEO: I can dress myself, you stupid cow.

LEO *throws the towel in* THERESE's *face with a triumphant hoot.* THERESE *steels herself not to react.*

THERESE: How about I make us a cup of tea, yeah?

LEO *grunts.*

Are you going to sulk now? I hate sulking.

LEO: And I hate bossy bossy-boots.

THERESE: I have to be bossy. Otherwise you'd lie up there in bed all day getting smashed, never eat and never wash.

LEO *mimics her nagging tone. There's a knock on the door.* THERESE *opens the door to a chirpy, smoothy guy, carrying a portfolio and a bottle of scotch.* GAVIN.

GAVIN: Hi! Gavin.

THERESE: Uh—hello—

GAVIN: Is Leo up and about? Figured I'd swing by for a surprise visit. Hope that's okay.

LEO: You making tea or not?

THERESE: Cheer up. You got a visitor. It's Gavin.

LEO: Who?

GAVIN *slaps* LEO *on the back with affectionate familiarity.*

GAVIN: Leo mate, how you going? [*To* THERESE] Me and Leo are old mates. [*To* LEO] Brought some pictures to show you—plus a little something.

LEO's *eyes fix on the scotch that* GAVIN *puts down nearby.*

LEO: Me and Gavin are old mates. Aren't we, mate?

LEO *throws an arm around* GAVIN.

GAVIN: Abso-bloody-lutely, Leo.

THERESE: I was just about to make a cup of tea.

GAVIN: Aww, wouldn't say no.

As THERESE *goes to make tea, she moves the scotch out of* LEO's *reach.*

THERESE: You're our first real visitor. Other than the guys who deliver groceries and the liquor shop stuff. Oh, I'm Therese, by the way.

GAVIN: You're new here, Therese.

THERESE: This is my sixth week.

LEO: They never last long, Gavin mate.

THERESE: I'm going to. You watch me.

LEO: She's a bossy-boots, this one.

GAVIN: [*to* THERESE] How is he today? Has he been—uh—?

GAVIN mimes guzzling booze.

THERESE: Yeah. I try to get him to cut it back—

She shrugs—it's hopeless.

GAVIN: Oh well… he's a naughty boy, sometimes, aren't you Leo?

LEO: Yep. Yep. I'm a naughty boy, mate.

GAVIN: Just as well you're so special.

LEO: [*to* THERESE] Hear that, bossy-boots? I'm special!

THERESE heads to the kitchen.

GAVIN: Few pencil drawings I wanted to show you—get your expert opinion on— Oh, before I get those out, do you wanna just sign a few of these for me, Leo mate?

LEO: Sure, mate. Got a pen?

GAVIN: I most surely do.

GAVIN pulls out blank pieces of thick paper and balances them so LEO can sign the bottom.

LEO: You know what, Miss Bossy? My signature is worth thousands of dollars. Salvador Dali did this, you know. [*To* GAVIN] She's stupid. Doesn't understand anything. [*He waves the hand holding the pen.*] This bit of me is worth a hundred thousand times more than the rest of my body put together.

GAVIN's pager beeps. He reads the display.

GAVIN: Oh, what? Wouldn't you bloody know it. Listen, Leo mate, I have to dash off. But I'll make some time to come back and show you those drawings.

LEO: No worries, mate. [*To* THERESE] Gavin's a busy bloke.

GAVIN: [*to* THERESE, *with a charming grin*] Unfortunately true. Thanks for making the tea, Therese—even if I can't stay to enjoy it. Catch you both soon.

    GAVIN *is out the door in smooth quick time.*

LEO: Gavin left his pen.

THERESE: Was he getting you to sign blank pieces of paper?

LEO: That wasn't paper. It was 600 gsm Arches.

THERESE: Whatever. Do you really know that bloke?

LEO: He was here once before. These pants are prickling me. You put the prickles in the washing machine.

THERESE: I don't and you know it. Was Gavin getting you to sign blank paper the other time he came?

LEO: Yeah.

THERESE: But apart from that you don't know him? Why did you say— ? Oh Leo!

LEO: Don't yell at me.

THERESE: I'm not yelling at you. I'm yelling at that bloke who's ripping you off!

LEO: What bloke? There's no bloke here.

THERESE: The bloke who was here a minute ago. Gavin.

LEO: I don't know any Gavin.

    LEO *shrinks away from* THERESE.

THERESE: You said he was an old mate but he's just some rip-off merchant! Bloody hell… He's ripping you off, Leo!

LEO: You're yelling at me. Stop yelling.

THERESE: I'm not yelling! I'm just— Oh…

    LEO *escapes out the door towards the bathroom. There's a knock on the front door.*

Quiet as a grave for six weeks and now it's like fucking Pitt Street.

    She opens the door to MARGO.

Oh. Hi. Leo! Margo's here to visit you!

MARGO: Don't bother. He hides if I turn up here. Looks like you're coping okay.

THERESE: No, no, pretty much okay.

MARGO: Has the carpenter arrived?

THERESE: No. But a tradesman's what we need. Whole wall fell off the bathroom the other day.

MARGO: The carpenter's coming to quote on a job. We're removing this panel. There's a mural underneath the layers of muck.

THERESE: Well, no carpenter's turned up.

> THERESE *darts across to look towards the bathroom for a sign of* LEO. MARGO *notices how frazzled* THERESE *looks.*

MARGO: Is something wrong?

THERESE: No—well—no.

MARGO: I realise this job must be stressful sometimes.

THERESE: Well, yeah.

MARGO: But since I hadn't heard, I assumed you were coping with things. Is there anything you want to—?

THERESE: Atchally I wanted to ask you about the liquor shop deliveries.

MARGO: Is there a problem? The account comes to my office and as far as I know—

THERESE: No problem with the paying. It's just—well, a whole box of booze delivered to the door every week...

MARGO: Leo orders it.

THERESE: But shouldn't someone try to—?

MARGO: I have tried to get him off it. Several times. It's hopeless. And in the end, it's his choice.

THERESE: I guess so... Have you told Leo about the wall? I mean, if you rip out part of his house, he'll go ballistic.

MARGO: I know. I'm sorry about that. But we don't have many options. His financial situation is very tight.

THERESE: Fair enough. I guess we'll manage. But aren't his paintings worth, like, megabucks?

MARGO: A Bailey reached a new record at auction last month.

THERESE: Yeah, so if he needs money, can't you just sell one?

MARGO: Leo doesn't own the paintings—well, very few now.

THERESE: So where did they all go?

MARGO: Squandered by him. Given away to buy love.

THERESE: So when a painting gets big money at the auction, it goes to—

MARGO: Whichever clever investor owns a valuable Bailey.

THERESE: There's one picture he goes on and on about.

MARGO: 'The Laughing Girl'.

THERESE: That's it.

MARGO: Much-loved, considered one of his best. It disappeared from the market years ago.

THERESE: Leo reckons it's been stolen.

MARGO: My theory is that some investor is holding 'The Laughing Girl' until Leo dies. It'll be worth considerably more when he's dead.

THERESE: I guess that must be it.

MARGO: Look, other members of the family might have stolen paintings over the years. But I think any money they've got is fair compensation for putting up with him.

THERESE: What about you?

MARGO: I don't touch his money and I don't subsidise him with one cent of mine.

THERESE: So—what—you manage his bank stuff?

MARGO: My task is to calculate the value of his remaining assets and divide that by the estimated number of months he'll live. If he lives longer than the medical projections, he can't afford to stay in this house.

THERESE: Shit… how can you talk about him like that? So fucking cold. I mean, I know Leo's hard work but he is your dad.

MARGO: Yes he is.

THERESE: He can't help it if he's cranky and mental and gives people the shits. That's what happens when you get old and sick.

MARGO: Don't you ever wonder why no friends or family come around here?

THERESE: I guess most people can't handle how gross old blokes can get.

MARGO: If you saw lonely, sick old people in a nursing home with no visitors, you'd be sympathetic, wouldn't you?

THERESE: Yeah, of course.

MARGO: I'd want to know what those old men and women did in their lives that made them end up alone and unloved.

THERESE: But you've gotta feel sorry for them.

MARGO: I feel sorry for the children who aren't visiting their toxic parents because I bet they've got bloody good reasons.

THERESE: I guess.

MARGO: Among the Leo Bailey wives and children, there's at least four nervous breakdowns, three substance abusers, two suicides and not one partridge in a fucking pear tree. All his life people made allowances because of the art.

THERESE: You mean, they let him get away with acting like a shit.

MARGO: It's done him no favours. He never learned to treat people decently. The carpenter's late. Can you make sure he finds this note?

> MARGO *leaves a note on the table and heads for the door.*

THERESE: No worries. And look, I'm sorry for being a stickybeak. I really want to keep this job and it's none of my business how— y'know...

> MARGO *signals goodbye and leaves.* THERESE *yells out to the bathroom.*

Leo! You can stop hiding! The Viper's gone! Shit, Leo... where are you?

> *She searches, puzzled not to find him. There's a knock at the door.* THERESE *runs towards it.*

Bugger you! Why did you run off? You scared the shit out of me!

> *She opens the door to see a guy wearing builder's gear.* KARL *is around thirty, gentle, polite.*

KARL: Sorry I'm late. It's tricky to find this place.

> THERESE *looks around* KARL *to peer down the street.*

Is this number twenty-eight? Margo Bailey?

THERESE: Eh? No. I mean, yes, this is number twenty-eight— Did you see a little guy running down the street?

KARL: Uh, no.

THERESE: He got out through a hole in the side fence. Ran away. He could've gone in any direction.

KARL: Is this your son who's run off?

THERESE: No, no, Leo's an old bloke. I wasn't yelling at him but he thought I was and now he's run away.

KARL: We could drive around in my truck and look for him if you—

THERESE: Trucks! Shit! What if he stumbles in front of some truck and gets squelched? I'm gonna get the sack.

KARL: Look—uh—could we ring someone?

THERESE: Who would you ring? He's not micro-chipped like a dog.

KARL: Police, I guess.

THERESE: No way. I'm allergic to cops. No bloody way.

KARL: Okay.

THERESE: Don't mean to bite your head off, mate.

KARL: Nah, nah. You're right. So you're not Margo Bailey?

THERESE: No. I'm the paid help, to look after the old guy. Who are you?

KARL: Oh. Sorry. Karl.

He offers his hand to shake but she's too frantic to notice.

I'm a builder—carpenter—well, odd-job guy. Ms Bailey asked me to come and quote on a small job.

THERESE: Oh, that's right. You're going to rip out the wall.

KARL: Well, not exactly rip it out.

THERESE *bellows out the door towards the bathroom.*

THERESE: Leo! Are you out hiding out there? If you're hiding, I'm gonna—! Deadset, Leo—I'll smack you so hard! [*She feels* KARL *staring at her.*] What?

KARL: Sorry?

THERESE: You're giving me the hairy eyeball. Reckon I'm doing a shithouse job, do ya?

KARL: No… I'm only—

THERESE: It's not easy looking after a guy like Leo, you know.

KARL: I'm sure it isn't. I wasn't—

THERESE: If you haven't been stuck looking after the old pisshead for six weeks like I have, you can't go around judging me, okay?

KARL: Oh, what… no… I wasn't. I'm just wondering what I can do to—

THERESE: And don't you say anything to her either. The daughter. About me losing him. Because I'm gonna find the little fucker.

The sound of a car honking outside. THERESE *peers out the front door.*

A taxi. What's he—? Leo!

She rushes outside, leaving KARL *there. He starts to organise his work gear but is distracted by the scene outside.* LEO *stumbles in, barefoot, bleeding from grazes on his head and hands, clutching the scotch bottle.*

KARL: Hello. Mr Bailey? Are you all right?

LEO: My shoes! That bastard taxi driver is holding my shoes hostage!

KARL: Oh—your shoes.

LEO: Yes! You go and rescue my shoes! Quickly!

LEO *collapses, moaning.* KARL *goes outside, passing* THERESE *as she rushes back in.*

THERESE: Are you going?

KARL: To get his shoes.

KARL *exits.*

THERESE: [*to* LEO] Oh, look at your head. I'll get something to clean you up.

She cleans up LEO*'s grazes. He pulls away, ouching like a little kid.*

LEO: Stupid mongrel taxi driver—I gave him the address I wanted to go to but he couldn't find his arse with both hands. Ow!

THERESE: Keep still. How did you hurt your head?

LEO: That fascist bruised my arm with his stinking sausage fingers!

THERESE: The taxi driver did this to you?

LEO: His fault.

THERESE: What did he do?

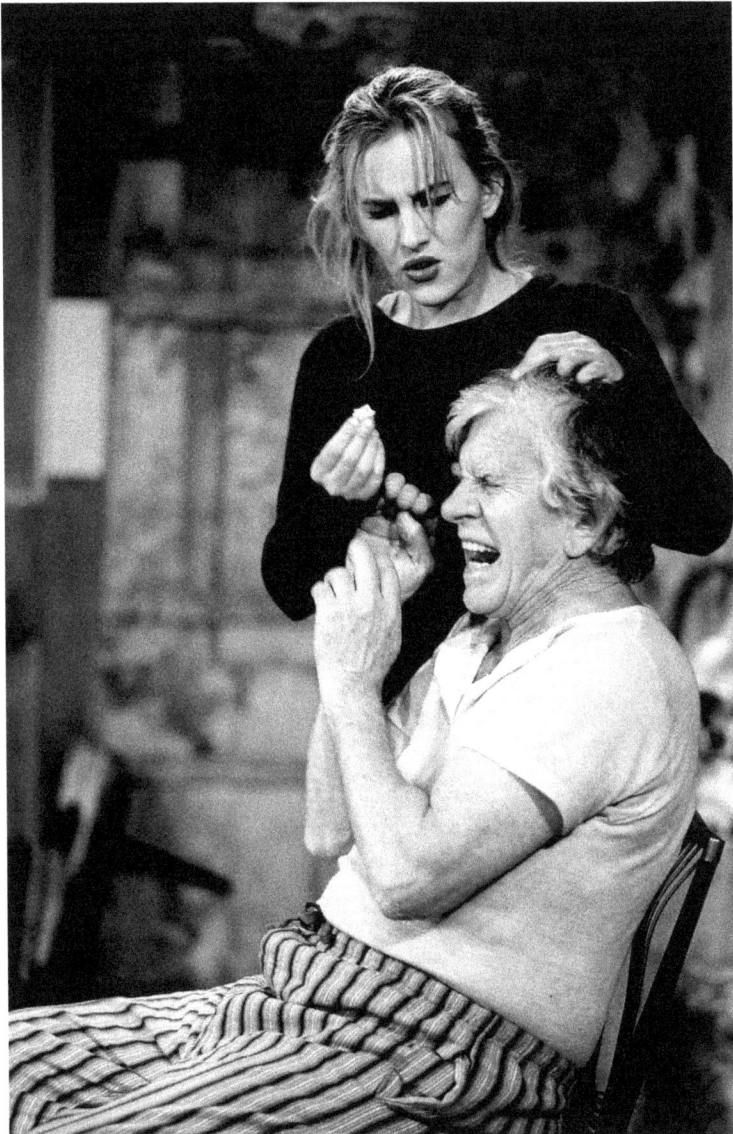

*Kate Mulvany as Therese and Martin Vaughan as Leo in the 2004
Griffin Theatre production. (Photo: Robert McFarlane)*

LEO: He was so stupid, I had to get out of the cab. That's why I fell over in the street.

THERESE: Well, that's not—

LEO: Then he kidnapped my shoes!

KARL enters as LEO *pulls away from* THERESE*'s first aid.*

Ow! Ow! She's trying to kill me!

THERESE: It's antiseptic. Stop being such a baby.

THERESE chases LEO *around the room to tend to his wounds.*

KARL: Look, umm, the cabbie seems pretty keen to get his fare.

LEO: Don't let him in my house! He's a Nazi!

THERESE: Just because he's got an accent doesn't mean—

LEO: He's a Nazi!

KARL: Actually, he's Hungarian.

THERESE: Whatever. The point is, he's not a Nazi.

KARL: He says he wants the money or he'll ring the police.

THERESE: The police?

LEO: Fascist mongrel. I paid the fare.

THERESE: How? You don't have any money.

KARL: He promised the driver a hundred-dollar tip. Then he tried to pay with this.

He produces a crumpled leaflet with a signature scrawled on the back and hands it to THERESE.

It's just his signature.

LEO snatches it from her hand and tears it into tiny pieces. He yells out the door:

LEO: *Heil Hitler! Heil Hitler,* you mongrel!

THERESE chases after LEO *with band-aids.*

THERESE: Stop it! Come here and let me—

LEO: Don't let the Nazi come in here!

KARL: Don't worry. He won't come inside. He's thinks you're both crazy people.

A couple more honks from the taxi outside.

THERESE: Why doesn't he piss off?

KARL: It might be a good idea just to give this guy his money and—

THERESE: Yeah, yeah, okay.

> *She now has* LEO *on the ground, sitting on him, while she gets band-aids on his cuts.*

Can you look in my purse? It's in the drawer.

> KARL *goes through the purse.*

LEO: What's he doing? Is he stealing?

THERESE: No. Stop wriggling.

LEO: Is he your husband?

THERESE: No.

> KARL *pulls notes out of the purse.*

KARL: There's forty here.

THERESE: That should cover it.

KARL: Well, no. The fare is fifteen plus there's the upholstery.

THERESE: Beg yours? Upholstery? Lie down, Leo, and stop doing that!

KARL: Apparently there's some blood on his upholstery. He wants fifty dollars.

THERESE: Fifty bucks!

KARL: Well, that's the standard cleaning fee. There's usually a little sticker on the dash.

LEO: I never saw his stinking fascist sticker.

THERESE: [*to* LEO] Keep still and let me fix you up.

KARL: Sixty-five in total. Have you got it?

THERESE: That's all I've got.

> LEO *is wailing and slapping* THERESE*'s hands away. The honking sound gets more insistent.*

Ohhh. Why doesn't he shut up? Why does he have to be so aggro?

LEO: You're hurting me! And what about my shoes? You have to pay the ransom for my shoes!

THERESE: Shoosh, Leo. I can't think. [*She bellows out the door.*] Shut the fuck up, you aggro dick!

KARL: He did say three minutes or he'd ring the police.

> THERESE *releases her hold on* LEO *who drops to the floor like a rag doll. She grabs the cash from* KARL *and stomps to the door.*

THERESE: Right. He can take this forty bucks and shove it up his arse.

> KARL *scoots round to block her exit.*

KARL: Well, y'know, maybe it'd be better if you didn't go out there. I mean, the taxi guy is pretty aggro—as you pointed out—and... Look, I've got the other twenty-five dollars on me. Maybe I should sort things out.

THERESE: But that bastard can't bully us into—

KARL: I'll go and talk to him. Is that okay?

> THERESE *shrugs—okay. She hands* KARL *the forty dollars and he exits.* THERESE *watches out the door.*

LEO: Is that man getting my shoes back?

THERESE: Can't tell from here.

> LEO *stumbles to a chair where he curls up in a ball.*

Oh, Leo, I was packing it for a minute there. Don't scare me like that again, okay?

> KARL *enters with Leo's shoes and gives them to* THERESE.

Thanks. And—y'know—thanks.

> *She hands the shoes to* LEO *who cradles them like a baby.*

Look, I can't pay you back the twenty-five bucks right now so—

KARL: When you can. [*He moves to face* LEO *directly.*] G'day. My name's Karl.

LEO: [*scrutinising him*] Karl. Hello, Karl.

THERESE: That's nice.

KARL: Sorry?

THERESE: People who come here—delivery guys and that—they talk to him like he's a vegetable. I'm Therese, by the way.

KARL: Hi, Therese.

THERESE: Sorry about before. Sorry if I was a bit—

KARL: No worries.

THERESE: Listen, Karl, do you have to start ripping out the wall right this minute?

KARL: Oh, I'm only measuring up today. The wall won't come down for a month, they said. It goes to the restorer and then to the auction house.

THERESE: A month. Beaudie.

KARL: Do you want me to come back another—?

THERESE: Nah, you're right. Measure away.

> KARL *starts measuring the wall.* LEO *groans in pain.*

What am I going to do with you, eh? Why did you run off?

LEO: I wanted to go out. Out.

THERESE: I'd take you out places except you get drunk and fall over and call taxi drivers Nazis.

LEO: He was a Nazi.

THERESE: He wasn't a Nazi. That's why we can't go out. I can't trust you to behave if you're pissed.

LEO: Prison. It's like prison, Karl. Can you hear how she talks to me?

THERESE: Leo, I'll do you a deal. You lay off the grog and I'll take you on outings.

LEO: Eh?

THERESE: We cancel the liquor shop delivery, everything. If you stay sober, we can—

LEO: Hear how she tricks me, Karl? Torturing me.

KARL: Sounds like a fair deal to me, Leo.

LEO: You reckon, Karl? Do you reckon it's fair?

KARL: I do.

THERESE: We can scoot all over the city—wherever you like. We got a deal?

> LEO *sulks and mutters.*

Beg yours? Couldn't hear that.

LEO: All right. Deal.

> LEO *stomps off in a sulk and then escapes out the front door.*

THERESE: Leo!

THERESE *picks up the scotch bottle left by* GAVIN *and chases after* LEO. KARL *measures up the wall.*

◆ ◆ ◆ ◆ ◆

SCENE THREE

KARL *has taken down the panel with the mural covered in papers and thrown paint. He's put new cladding in its place and is doing the finishing touches.*

THERESE *and* LEO *come in the front door.* LEO *is sober, dressed in clothes rather than pyjamas, and is looking better.*

LEO: Karl! Still at it! [*To* THERESE] I told you he'd still be here if we got back by three o'clock.

KARL: So where did you guys end up deciding to go today?

LEO: Ten pin bowling. A fine sport for mind, body and spirit.

LEO *mimes a bowling action with a flourish.*

THERESE: The mongrel beats me every time. He's such a lucky dog— he drops the ball and it rolls into perfect position.

LEO: It's skill, girlie. Not luck. [*He scrutinises the wall.*] How many days has Karl been here?

THERESE: Oh—uh—

KARL: Four.

LEO: Are they paying you by the hour?

KARL: No.

LEO: Bloody long time for a job like this.

THERESE: Well, I guess Karl's very thorough.

LEO: So! What's on the agenda for tomorrow? More bowling?

LEO *does his bowling action again.*

KARL: I thought you'd wanna go round the art galleries, Leo.

LEO *does a flamboyant wail and rolls his head around.*

THERESE: No way.

LEO: Art! Ha! I don't want to go anywhere near art.

THERESE: We stick to movies, museums, ferry rides.

LEO: Movies tomorrow.

THERESE: Sure. We can have a look at what's on.

LEO grabs a newspaper from Therese's bag and wrestles it to find the movie ads.

How are your ankles?

LEO: Still attached to my feet. Don't fuss.

THERESE: It's a long walk up from the ferry.

LEO: [*to* KARL] She has a thing about my ankles.

But his ankles are aching and he sinks into the armchair.
THERESE takes Leo's shoes off while he peers at the newspaper ads.

THERESE: He still gets this fluid building up in his belly and in his legs. Makes him uncomfortable. Ascites, it's called. Alcos get it 'cos their liver doesn't make some enzyme.

KARL looks at her, surprised.

I have to know this stuff so I don't sound like such a dumbo when I talk to the docs. Dunno why I'm boring you with it.

KARL: I guess because—

THERESE: Because it's been my whole life for the last two months and I've got no one else to tell.

THERESE and KARL realise that LEO has dozed off.

KARL: I was thinking—when I saw him again at the start of this week— well, he definitely looks better than a month ago—I mean, better since you got him off the grog.

THERESE: We have good days and bad days. But when he was boozing every day was a bad day.

KARL: Withdrawing from booze can't be easy on a person's body.

THERESE: Once we got through the vomiting and the shakes, I thought we'd be okay. But now he just goes quiet. I'm not sure what's going through his mind sometimes.

KARL: Do you think he could be a bit lonely? I mean, for his old mates.

THERESE: I phoned up the list of old friends. They all hate his guts. One bloke—you could hear in his voice, the poor guy was still really, like, wounded.

KARL: What about his family? Don't they—?

THERESE: Don't come near him. Leo reckons they're all monsters.

KARL: They might just seem that way to him.

THERESE: Maybe. Anyway, I reckon he helped make them into monsters. Even if he is famous.

KARL: I looked up in a book and it reckons Leo Bailey's one of the greatest living Australian artists. I can't imagine having an imagination like that. I just see what I see—what's in front of me, you know. But for a person like Leo, it's different. Must be incredible to have a brain like that.

THERESE: Yeah. That's why people think there's a different set of rules for a guy like Leo.

KARL: Is that what you think?

THERESE: No. I don't think those— [*referring to the paintings*] — gave him the right to be a total dickhead all his life. Then again, there's plenty of destructive bastards out there who aren't great artists.

KARL: Reckon.

> THERESE *and* KARL *smile. Then both quickly feel awkward.*

THERESE: Anyway, it's not my job to worry about all that. It's my job to look after the poor old bugger he is now. I watch him when he's asleep sometimes and I say to myself, 'Therese, he's this famous big-deal artist and look at him. Look at him.'

> KARL *sees* THERESE *smile affectionately at* LEO. KARL *moves closer.*

KARL: He's lucky to have you.

THERESE: [*ducking away from* KARL] I'm lucky to have this job. Looking after a scungy old drunk is deadset the best job I'm gonna get.

> *She gives an embarrassed laugh.* KARL *hastily packs up his tools.*

You're finished up?

KARL: Yep.

THERESE: Leo's gonna miss you. He liked having you round here the last week.

KARL: Yeah, well, I've—

THERESE: So you got a new job to go on to?

KARL: Little jobs like this one.

THERESE: You don't, like, renovate whole houses or that?

KARL: Used to. I had a business with another bloke. Business went under.

THERESE: Not enough work around?

KARL: We had plenty of work. I didn't pay enough attention to the books. Left it up to the other bloke.

THERESE: What—and he mucked it up?

KARL: Took the money and disappeared. Bali.

THERESE: Yeah? What an arsehole!

KARL: He was my best mate since kindy.

THERESE: Oh. Therese's big mouth. Sorry. I just meant—

KARL: Why should you apologise? I guess he probably was an arsehole. Took me a while to figure it out. Still can't get my head round it.

THERESE: So are you gonna take him to court, or whatever, to get the money?

KARL: Nah. No point. This kind of work suits me anyway. I'll get the debts paid off soon and have nothing hanging over me.

LEO *jolts awake, upset.*

THERESE: Leo, hey. It's okay. Bad dream, eh?

LEO: Coldness was creeping up from my toes. I was dying, I was dying!

THERESE: Hang on a sec.

She makes a show of feeling for a pulse.

Nup. Definitely not dead.

She laughs, then notices that LEO *is still upset.*

You know what, Leo? I'm going to give you a shave. Hot towels, aftershave, the works. How about that? [*She runs around getting the stuff she needs.*] A shave cheers him up when he's upset. Like when that nurse came in last Sunday.

LEO: Stupid, squawking bloody woman.

THERESE: You did try to bite a piece out of her ear. [*To* KARL] The respite nurses upset him and Leo turns ugly on them.

LEO: I don't want them in my house.

THERESE: Don't get in a tizz. I'm cancelling them. No more Sunday nurses. Just me from now on.

LEO: Good. And Karl.

THERESE: Well, no. Karl's finished up here. He won't be coming back.

LEO *makes a moan of distress.*

We're gonna miss Karl, aren't we?

KARL: Well, if you ever need someone to fix that bathroom wall...

THERESE: What, and do Leo out of his cheap thrills seeing me in the nuddy?

KARL: Yeah, fair enough.

THERESE: Oh—I wasn't saying we wouldn't want you to come back and fix stuff.

KARL: Yeah. Don't worry about it—

THERESE: There's no money to pay for repairs but.

KARL: Sure. I understand.

THERESE: I left messages a coupla times with his daughter, about getting things fixed. No go.

KARL: I wasn't pushing you for work. Forget it.

KARL *and* THERESE *are both silent, knowing they've mucked it.*

LEO: Why can't Karl just visit anyway?

KARL: Oh... well—I could—uh—

THERESE: Karl's too busy to be dropping round to visit us.

KARL: Oh, y'know, when I'm driving back from a job—

THERESE: You see? He's got to drive halfway across Sydney for work. He's busy. Anyway he wouldn't want to visit a complaining old wet-brain and a big-mouth slag.

KARL: Eh? No—

THERESE: You see? No. He wouldn't want to.

KARL: I guess you don't really want people turning up here out of the blue. I'll—uh…

> KARL *grabs his gear to go.*

LEO: I do. I like people turning up out of the blue.

THERESE: Leo does love visitors but you don't want to be—

KARL: I get the message. I'll get out your way.

THERESE: Oh. Okay.

KARL: Thanks for everything. [*To* LEO] You look after Therese.

LEO: It's a full-time job.

> THERESE *follows* KARL *towards the door.*

THERESE: Thanks for being friendly to Leo. I'm paid to be nice to him. But you were nice to him for no reason. Some kind of weird bastard, are ya?

KARL: Guess I must be.

THERESE: I was only joking. I didn't mean—

KARL: Sure. [*To* LEO] See you round then, eh mate.

LEO: Round like a rissole.

> THERESE *watches* KARL *go and curses herself under her breath. Then she spins back and grabs the things for the shave.*

THERESE: Let's get cracking with this.

LEO: He's a decent man.

THERESE: What?

LEO: Karl. He's a good man. A bit lost.

THERESE: I don't know. I guess so…

LEO: He notices things. He sees people. You look at his eyes. Except now you can't look at his eyes because he's gone forever.

> THERESE *drapes towels round* LEO*'s shoulders, combs his hair back, lathers up his face.*

THERESE: Cheer up, misery-guts. You're gonna get the full Therese Laurence beauty treatment and after, we'll see what's on the telly-box.

LEO: Am I getting hot towels?

THERESE: Yeah yeah, don't start whingeing.

> *She starts shaving him.* LEO *obediently holds still for her.*

Lip.

> LEO *tightens his upper lip.*

Good on ya.

> *She lathers up more soap. When she looks up,* LEO *is staring at her. She cups his face in her hands.*

You're a gorgeous thing, you know.

LEO: Am I?

THERESE: Yeah. You are. Gorgeous.

LEO: I always used to think I looked like a troll.

THERESE: I don't even know what trolls look like.

LEO: The paintings made beautiful women sleep with me. It was the paintings.

THERESE: Come on, don't get yourself upset.

> LEO *grabs her hand to stop the shaving.*

LEO: Do you understand?

THERESE: I understand about feeling ugly, yeah. You should consider yourself a lucky bastard. If I could do some fabulous thing that'd make people love me, I'd be out there doing my fabulous thing and not standing here shaving you. Whoops—sudsy bit dripping.

> *She dries a soapy bit.* LEO*'s face crumples into tears.*

Leo... I was only joking around.

> LEO *shakes his head, his face contorted with tears.*

You got pain somewhere? Is it your knees?

> LEO *can't answer.*

Tell me and I'll fix it.

LEO: You can't fix it. It's everything.

THERESE: Everything what?

LEO: I've started remembering things. You can't fix what I've done.

THERESE: Oh. You're remembering things you feel bad about?

LEO: Shame. I'm talking about shame. You don't understand. How could you know about shame?

THERESE: That's where you're dead wrong. I know about shame.

LEO: No, no, no… you're young. Too young. You can't understand.

THERESE: You reckon? You'd be amazed the amount of shameful shit you can fit in by my age if you get started early enough.

LEO: Tell me.

THERESE: Shoplifting when I was eleven. Smashing up bus shelters at twelve. Helping my boyfriend do break-and-enters by the time I was thirteen. Fourteen, got caught behind the service station doing blow-jobs for cash.

LEO: Did your parents disown you?

THERESE: 'It's not Therese. It's those no-hopers she hooks up with.' That's no excuse but. One time, this friend of Mum's gave me a job at her hairdresser's. Unbelievably nice of this lady—she didn't have to help out little rough-head Therese. Talked about getting me into tech to do the apprenticeship. Giving me a chance. So what did Therese do? Ripped the nice lady off—cleaned out the till and then helped my friends trash the shop for fun.

LEO: Why?

THERESE: Out to impress my mates. Plus I was pissed off—like the world owed me something and I was gonna take what I deserved. You get an urge to smash things—like it's evidence you exist. Evidence you did something.

LEO: Did you get caught?

THERESE: No. Next day, I go back there and the lady's cleaning up the broken glass and crying and she's apologising to me about the job being off. I felt like scum—I even cried. She goes, 'Oh, you're so sweet, Therese.' I never had the guts to say anything. That was years ago but I can feel my face burning just thinking about it. Hunh… You're the first person I ever told about that. How about that, Leo? [*She fusses with the towels to avoid his gaze.*] The first time I was up for something in adult court, I saw my—

LEO: In court for what?

THERESE: Forging and uttering—that's dud cheques. But stealing mostly— break-and-enter, warehouses and that.

LEO: Stealing money for drugs?

THERESE: No. Not for me anyway. Usually to keep some useless dickhead boyfriend happy. I got perfect radar for the nastiest creeps on the face of the earth. In court, I spotted Mum and Dad sitting in the audience part. They looked at me like—not angry or anything—but so sad and worried and disappointed... I never looked at them. I could still feel their eyes on me but. When I got out of jail the first time, I disappeared myself from Mum and Dad. Made it so they couldn't find me. I don't like the way I am. Haven't seen them for nearly six years.

She washes LEO's *face gently with a cloth.*

Some memory oozes up and eats away at your guts, eh. You know what I think about sometimes? When I'm in the shower, I tip my head back and I let the water run down my face and my neck and I imagine if the water could wash it all away...

LEO: The shame.

THERESE: Yeah. Wash away every bad thing I ever did. Start again, clean.

LEO *stares at her, wretched.* THERESE *bundles him up in towels.*

So, Mr Troll: how about those hot towels, yeah?

SCENE FOUR

Daytime. The house is apparently empty.

There's a knock at the door, then the sound of MARGO's *voice.*

MARGO: [*offstage*] Hello? Ms Laurence?

MARGO *enters and takes the chance to have a stickybeak, maybe finding a folder of papers somewhere.*

THERESE: [*offstage, yelling from bathroom*] Bugger off! I saw you spying!

MARGO *jumps, feeling caught out. Then* LEO *runs in from the bathroom. He's too focused on watching* THERESE *in the bathroom to notice* MARGO. *He giggles, hopping around, more spritely than* MARGO *has seen him.* THERESE *comes stomping in from the bathroom in a bathrobe.*

You're an old pervert, Leo—spying on me in the shower. It's not on. Oh.

MARGO: I'm sorry. I did knock.

THERESE: Sorry. I didn't hear it.

MARGO: I thought no one was home. I'm sorry.

THERESE: No worries. Let me just...

> *She secures the bathrobe.* LEO *is shuffling backwards to escape up the stairs.* THERESE *grabs him and makes him stay.*

Did you say hello to Margo?

> LEO *stays in the room but keeps well away from* MARGO.

Hey—d'you want a cup of tea? We just put the kettle on, didn't we Leo?

MARGO: No, thanks. [*She gets a bundle of large papers out of her brief-case.*] I can't stay. I just wanted to drop off these pages.

LEO: I won't sign anything.

THERESE: [*to calm him down*] Leo.

MARGO: There's nothing to be signed. It's the introduction to the new book about Leo.

THERESE: Oh, we're so excited about the new book, aren't we Leo? I reckon it'd be nice if you got Margo a cup of tea.

MARGO: Oh, I don't think so.

THERESE: He can do it. [*To* LEO] Go on.

> *With an enthusiastic shove from* THERESE, LEO *exits to get tea.* MARGO *lays the pages on the table.*

MARGO: I told the publisher I'd personally deliver the page proofs to Leo. Not that he'll read them.

THERESE: He might. It's a while since you've seen him and in the last two months, he's got a lot better. You and Leo can have a cup of tea and a yack about the new book.

> MARGO *sits down.*

That's a lovely jacket.

MARGO: Oh. Thank you.

THERESE: You always look so stylish, so classy.

MARGO: It's just money.

THERESE: You could spray thousands of bucks at me with a high-pressure hose and I'd never look classy.

THERESE *barks a laugh and* MARGO *smiles.*

MARGO: I just have to dress this way for my job.

THERESE: Listen, um, I know you do a lot for Leo.

MARGO: Me? The Viper?

THERESE: I don't think you're a viper. You're the only one out of his whole family who even bothers to come round.

MARGO: You wouldn't call me the 'nice one', would you?

THERESE: A lot of people would've just gone, 'Oh, I've had it with the old dickhead', and cut him off. It's amazing you've stuck around.

MARGO: You've stuck at this job much longer than anyone else. Apart from the Leo problem, people don't like the living in.

THERESE: Like living in a minimum security prison.

MARGO: Well, yes, it must feel very restrictive.

THERESE: Listen—I want to be straight with you. Before I came here, I was in some trouble.

MARGO: Oh… unless it's relevant to Leo's care, you don't have to tell me anything.

THERESE: I was in jail.

THERESE *waits for a response.*

MARGO: A horrible experience, I imagine.

THERESE: Yeah. Well, it was, yeah. One day, month before I got out, I looked around the dining hall at the women a bit older than me. In my head, I go, 'Do you want to end up looking like them, Therese?' And out loud, I go, 'No, I don't.' I made a vow to myself. To keep out of trouble from now on. To be good.

MARGO: Good.

LEO *appears with a tray of tea things.*

THERESE: Try my best anyway. So in a weird way it turns out this job is right for me. Because of it being restricted, I mean. It helps hold me in the place I'm trying to be.

LEO: Shall I be mother?

> LEO *chuckles at this idea and pours the tea.* MARGO *takes her tea from him.*

MARGO: Thanks.

LEO: Sorry about the flaky bits floating on top.

MARGO: That's fine.

> LEO *shrinks away.* THERESE *urges him to sit with them.*

LEO: I won't sign any of her papers.

THERESE: Leo. You don't realise how much stuff Margo does for you, organising things.

MARGO: [*to* THERESE] Really—don't waste your breath.

THERESE: No, well, he should think about it. Margo doesn't have to do the stuff she does for you and she's not ripping you off and—

LEO: [*proudly to* MARGO] I'm off the booze. Off the booze for— [*To* THERESE] How long?

THERESE: Eleven weeks.

MARGO: Well, that's very good.

LEO: My liver—Therese, tell about my liver.

THERESE: His liver function test improved heaps.

LEO: Doctor reckons my heart's sturdy and I could last another ten years!

THERESE: If you stay off alcohol and give your ulcers a chance to heal up and you—

LEO: [*to* MARGO] Ten years. [*To* THERESE] She thought I was gonna cark it any day. She's worried now. Look at her face.

THERESE: That's a horrible thing to say, Leo. I bet Margo's stoked you're better.

> *There's a knock on the door.* LEO *rushes to answer it.*

MARGO: Are you expecting someone?

THERESE: Uh—no. We never get visitors.

> LEO *opens the door to see* KARL, *holding timber pieces and a pile of glass louvres. He also brings in a small window*

wrapped in a dropsheet and leaves that bundle by the door.

LEO: Karl! I thought I'd never lay eyes on you again before I die.

KARL: Yeah, well… You're looking good, mate.

LEO: Welcome to my home. Welcome.

KARL: Therese is still looking after you then?

LEO: Yes, yes. She said we'd never see you again. But I knew you'd come back. Come in. *Entrez la porte.* [*In a sudden panic*] Oh, you're not here to hack out another piece of my house, are you?

KARL: No, mate. Relax. Dropped in because I brought something. [*To* THERESE] G'day. These are for you.

He hands THERESE *the timber pieces and glass louvres like he's handing her a bunch of flowers.*

Leftovers on a demolition site. Thought you could fix the louvre window in the bathroom.

THERESE: Oh. Yeah. Thanks.

KARL and THERESE are both stuck there awkwardly. LEO drags KARL by the arm.

[*To* MARGO] Karl's the builder who did that wall.

MARGO: Oh, right. Hello.

KARL: G'day.

MARGO: You finished the work on the wall some weeks ago, didn't you?

KARL: Yeah. I just stopped by to drop off— Got something else here too—

KARL indicates the bundled-up window.

MARGO: There isn't money available to do more building work on this house.

KARL: Sorry? Oh no, I'm not after work. I came across some leftover materials to help out Leo and—

LEO: Karl's a good bloke.

KARL: Look… uh, you're in the middle of something… I should get going.

LEO: Karl—the door in my bedroom—keeps jamming on the floor.

KARL: Probably swelled up in that rain. I could plane a bit off it for you.

LEO: Marvellous! Right now!

> LEO *grabs* KARL's *arm to drag him upstairs.*

THERESE: Stay here. Margo's visiting.

MARGO: Go on, Leo. You can go.

> LEO *scuttles upstairs with* KARL.

That's a record.

THERESE: Beg yours?

MARGO: That's longest he's stayed in a room with me without outright abuse. Plus the health improvements. Wow.

THERESE: Oh, well, we're not there yet. But I'm hoping if he stays off the grog, I can get him connecting with people a bit more.

MARGO: Ms Laurence—

THERESE: Therese.

MARGO: Therese, be careful you don't get your hopes up too high. He's been off the booze before. I must admit, never for this long—

THERESE: This time he's really broken through, I reckon. He's starting to face up to things. And now he'll have time, maybe years and years, to work on it.

MARGO: If it is years and years, I'm not sure what that's going to mean.

THERESE: I guess, but that's exciting in a way.

MARGO: For one thing, his money won't last that long. I have to think about how I'm going to—

THERESE: Yes, I know you handle all that and it's fantastic that you've hung in there. It shows that you must care about him. More than his other children anyway.

MARGO: Well, the younger children could walk away because he had less to do with them growing up.

THERESE: You could walk away now but you don't.

MARGO: I have tried to. Maintaining the excommunication of Leo cost me too much emotional energy. Now, I do what's needed and what's fair.

THERESE: I can see that.

MARGO: But, Therese, it takes a certain stamina. My stamina is not unlimited.

THERESE: Sure, I can get why you'd be sick of him but things can be different now. That's what I'm saying—

MARGO: I only survive around him with some distance and self-protection.

THERESE: But he's changing. I wish you could see.

MARGO: I have seen. I've seen how he can hurt people. I've seen it happen over and over. People would get drawn into Leo's orbit—it could be exhilarating, a wild ride. But in the end, they'd get obliterated by it. That's why I want to warn you not to—

THERESE: But you're talking about years ago. He's getting clearer in his head every week. Now there'll be time for you two to maybe reconnect. I'd so love it if that could happen.

MARGO *shrugs.*

MARGO: I'm just saying you should be careful.

THERESE: Me? I'll be okay.

MARGO: This house—it's already disintegrating. Do you really think this place will hold together for much longer?

THERESE: We'll manage.

MARGO: Anyway, I might head off.

THERESE: Oh no, stay. Leo'll come down in a sec.

MARGO: No, I think I'll go.

MARGO *heads for the door.* THERESE *rushes after her.*

THERESE: Hey—you should come with us on one of our outings.

MARGO: No.

THERESE: No, fair enough. Too much to start off. Better if you just drop by some time.

MARGO: We'll see. 'Bye, Therese.

THERESE: 'Bye. See you soon.

MARGO *leaves.*

[*Calling upstairs*] Leo! She's gone! Come down! She left the book stuff here for you!

LEO *comes downstairs, followed by* KARL.

LEO: She wants to steal my house.

THERESE: No, she doesn't.

LEO *moans to himself.*

Don't go all miserable on me. What a top day! You and Margo had a chat. She was really impressed with how you're going. Plus Karl's come back to visit you. Big lovely surprise. You should tell Karl the news about the book.

LEO *groans and makes a dismissive gesture.*

A fancy new book with lots of Leo's pictures in it.

KARL: Yeah? It'll be great for you to see all those paintings.

LEO *makes a farting noise.*

THERESE: Hey, don't be rude to Karl, sulky-bum. What about 'The Laughing Girl' one?

LEO *sulks.*

You'd like to see 'The Laughing Girl' in the new book, wouldn't you?

More silent sulking from LEO.

Well, I'd like to see it.

LEO *sighs and wanders outside.*

He comes over dark every now and then. Now he's sober, he's got forty years worth of stuff to sort through. His brain's processing it for the first time. We started making a list.

KARL: A list?

THERESE *grabs a folder to show* KARL—*the folder* MARGO *had a stickybeak at earlier.*

THERESE: When Leo remembers someone he dumped on, we add their name to the list. We're working through it, writing letters.

KARL: Sorry, I'm not with you.

THERESE: Apology letters. Leo tells me what he did to each person and I tell him how lousy he should feel. We give them a rating out of ten.

KARL: And what are these people supposed to do when they get the letters?

THERESE: Well, that doesn't matter. We're doing this so it isn't all one big, solid pile of Leo-was-a-bastard. 'Cos that paralyses a person.

Then he just slumps in the chair muttering 'shame, shame'. But with the letters, it feels like he's chipping away at the pile.

KARL: What about his ex-wives and his kids—have they got letters?

THERESE: We're working up to that.

KARL: I guess the letter-writing wasn't in your job description.

THERESE: Nuh. The job was supposed to be 'water the houseplant'. But you know what? I'm good at this job. Being a big-mouth scrag is good for something. [*She bellows outside.*] Leo! You gonna drink this tea before it's stone cold?

LEO: [*coming in*] Stop screeching at me, you harpie.

THERESE: Ah. He's cheered up.

KARL: I got something else for you, Leo.

> *He takes the dropsheet wrapping off the window—a leadlight window with richly-coloured glass.*

Found this in a house they were tearing down. It'll fit where the smashed one goes. Check it out with the light.

> *He props up the window so the light shines through it.*

The pattern's different but the colours are pretty much the same as the old one, don't you reckon?

> LEO *looks at the window, overcome.*

Leo? You okay?

LEO: Thank you, Karl. Thank you. The colours are the same, yes. My father had the set of windows made and sent to New Guinea by boat. When you sat in the front parlour in the afternoon, the light would come through the windows and make red and yellow shapes on the white tablecloth.

> LEO *goes into a dreamy state staring at the window.*

THERESE: [*whispering to* KARL] Thank you.

KARL: Do you want me to help you fit the louvres?

> KARL *indicates the timber and glass pieces he brought.*

THERESE: You better. Ta. I wouldn't have a clue.

> THERESE *and* KARL *head for the bathroom.* LEO *is still mesmerised by the window.*

LEO: Did you see what Karl brought me?

THERESE: Yeah. It's beautiful, Leo.

LEO: Is it my birthday?

THERESE: Not yet. Three weeks till your birthday.

LEO: Three weeks!

THERESE: I know that seems ages to wait. But don't worry. I'll figure out a really special way to celebrate.

THERESE *follows* KARL *into the bathroom to fix the window.*

LEO *stares at the leadlight window, then closes his eyes and sighs, transported.*

Then, from the bathroom, he hears THERESE *laughing and turns to watch her.*

LEO *runs to pick up a biro from one of his hiding places. With all his strength, he yanks at a wall of the house until a chunk of cladding breaks off.*

He positions himself so he can see into the bathroom. He tries to draw on the cladding with the biro. His hand shakes too much and he curses himself. He uses the other hand to steady the wrist of his drawing hand.

Washed over by the warmly-coloured light from the window, LEO *focuses on* THERESE. *He can hear her laugh every now and then as he draws.*

END OF ACT ONE

ACT TWO

SCENE ONE

Evening. There are balloons and other decorations around the house. Loud upbeat music blasts out of a CD player. THERESE *dances, singing along, as she brings out two brightly-wrapped presents.*

There's a knock on the door. She dances over to open it and then dances back in, beckoning KARL *to follow.*

KARL *holds out an armload of lining boards as an offering.*

KARL: These are for you.

THERESE: Hang on. [*She dances across to turn the music right down.*] Hi!

KARL: Uh—hi. Lining boards. Thought you could use them to replace the busted ones upstairs.

THERESE: Thanks. Great. You're a legend, Karl.

KARL: You're in a good mood.

THERESE: Scary, eh.

> KARL *puts another wrapped present beside the other two.*

KARL: Where's the birthday boy?

THERESE: [*calling upstairs*] Leo! Come down! You're beautiful enough! You were supposed to help me with the chopping!

> LEO *appears at the top of the stairs.*

LEO: Hear that, Karl? The harpie's making me cook my own birthday dinner.

> LEO *has spruced himself up, wearing a bow tie and waistcoat. He parades down the stairs.* THERESE *wolf-whistles.*

THERESE: Worth the wait, baby!

KARL: Happy birthday, Leo. Looking sharp.

LEO: I know.

KARL: Looking fit too.

LEO: Ooh, yeah. So fit I'm dangerous.

KARL: Glad to see it.

LEO: She's glad to see you. She was talking about you all week. 'Don't forget Karl's coming to your birthday dinner.'

> KARL *and* THERESE *blush, awkward.*

THERESE: Hey, Leo, I thought you were hanging out to tell Karl about the other week.

LEO: We've been having adventures!

THERESE: Go on. Tell him.

LEO: I'm a wet-brain. You do it.

THERESE: Oh. Okay. Well, there was this day Leo and me went to the movies—

LEO: Forget the movie. Get to the good part.

THERESE: Okay, Lord Muck. We get out of the movies and we head across town to the Botanical Gardens. It's lunchtime in the city—

LEO: People thick on the footpath, pushing and shoving.

THERESE: So I'm trying to make a little channel for Leo to fit through without getting walloped. Then he suddenly announces—

LEO: [*dancing around*] I need to take a leak.

THERESE: He does that—hangs on like a little kid until he's absolutely busting.

LEO: [*laughing*] Big emergency.

THERESE: 'Let's try in here', I say, and we go into the nearest office block. It's one of those huge buildings with the foyer that's all granite walls going right up.

LEO: Like the tomb of the Great Pharaoh.

THERESE: Makes you feel like a tiny maggot crawling along the bottom. Because it's lunchtime, all the lifts are running hot.

LEO: Ding ding ding.

THERESE: Spewing out these office workers in their suits acting like everything they do is more important than the rest of us but we wouldn't understand it. In the foyer—

LEO: Oh, let me tell about the bloke.

THERESE: Yeah, get this...

LEO: There's a concierge.

THERESE: Sitting at a glass and chrome desk.

LEO: With a little sign that says 'concierge'.

THERESE: Smirk on his face like his shit doesn't smell.

> LEO *roars with laughter, adoring* THERESE.

'Excuse me, is there a men's on this floor?'

LEO: She said it just like that. Polite.

THERESE: Mr Concierge looks down at us like we're some colourful fungus he'd like to hose off the shiny granite floor.

LEO: [*as the concierge*] 'Do you have an appointment in the building?'

THERESE: 'In a way, yeah', I say, 'My friend's bladder has an urgent appointment with your toilet.'

> LEO *loves that bit.*

So the guy goes—

LEO: 'Look, uh, madame—look, uh—'

THERESE: Just like that—like I smell bad.

LEO: Which she didn't.

THERESE: I go, 'No, how about you look, mate—unless you want him to relieve himself all over your shiny floor, I reckon you should point us in the direction of the gents quick smart.'

LEO: And that's just what he did. [*He pats* THERESE.] She was brilliant!

THERESE: If that wanker knew that he'd just met the famous Leo Bailey, he'd be all over him like a rash.

LEO: But he just thought it was some old derro!

THERESE: Some old derro gatecrashing the gents.

> *She and* LEO *share a smile.* LEO *is wriggling around.*

Do you need to go now? Go.

LEO: Tell him about the picture.

THERESE: I'm going to.

> LEO *exits to the bathroom.*

KARL: What picture?

THERESE: Oh, well... After I send Leo off to the gents, I sit down on this black leather couch. Mr Concierge's giving me the greasy eyeball like I'm going to steal the couch any second. Had a gutful of that, so I swivel round and face the other wall. Whoomp. There it is. This painting. It's enormous—maybe the size of that whole wall. It's one of Leo's—I saw a little section of it on a book cover. But that's not it. I mean, that's not why it hits me. The faces in the painting—the faces are just so—beautiful's not the word. People say 'beautiful' but that doesn't… It's like there's a light inside the painting shining directly on me, filling me up, sending an electric charge through my blood into every tiny cell of me. [*She stops, embarrassed.*] I know, you reckon that sounds—

KARL: No, no, I don't.

THERESE: Anyway, I'm looking at the painting. I know the snotty concierge is still staring. I can hear the ding ding of the lifts. I can still feel the cold air from the granite walls. But it's like a parallel universe I can see and hear but real faint. By the time Leo comes back out, I can't move. 'I need to sit for a minute, Leo.' So he sits beside me and looks up at the painting too.

KARL: Christ—what was going through Leo's head when he looked at that picture?

THERESE: I don't know. Did his own painting blow him away too? Or did he think about what he ate for dinner the day he finished it? Or maybe his brain's so shot—

KARL: —he didn't even remember painting it.

THERESE: Yeah… But y'know, it doesn't matter. The picture's more than him. It's bigger than all that stuff. The last week, I've been making Leo go to art galleries and insurance company foyers with me. I can tell you where every one of Leo's paintings is in Sydney— the ones people can see without owning them, that is. Leo paints ordinary stuff and ordinary people but his picture'll make them look special—make them beautiful and glowing and— But it's not tizzying things up. It's like Leo can see the specialness inside a thing so when a person looks at the painting they can see it too.

KARL *smiles to see her so transported. She laughs.*

Shit—yacking on like a lunatic and I'm running late!

THERESE *dashes around, getting ready.* LEO *comes back in.*

LEO: Therese is going to start a new life.

THERESE: Don't you make fun of me, Leo.

LEO: I'm not. I'm telling Karl. She found a brochure.

KARL: A brochure on how to start a new life?

THERESE: No, no. It was one of those pamphlets about adult education courses.

LEO: It was a sign from God!

KARL: An adult education brochure was a sign from God?

LEO: Why was that brochure on the train seat at exactly the right time for Therese to find it? Because it was a sign from God!

KARL: You never know.

LEO: You should've seen her, Karl—going through that brochure, putting big red circles round things.

THERESE: Just some courses I'd like to do.

LEO: History, languages, astronomy, fine art. And she's had the atlas out.

THERESE: I was thinking I might go overseas—I mean, when I've got some money.

LEO: Therese's new life!

THERESE *is embarrassed but exhilarated by the idea.*

Mind you, Karl—Therese's new life can't happen until after I'm dead. Dead as a door knob.

THERESE: Hey—I don't want any talk like that today. Today's a good day. Right?

LEO: Right.

LEO *nudges* KARL, *winks, and then roars with laughter.*

KARL: I wouldn't mind getting hold of a brochure on how to start a new life. Made a stuff-up of my old one.

THERESE: Wasn't your fault. That bastard friend ripped off your business. You shouldn't be so surprised that people can act like arseholes.

KARL: Mum always reckoned when I'd come home from school and some kid had been mean, I'd be confused—baffled—like I couldn't believe it. I don't see the nasty streaks in people. It's like a frequency

I can't hear or a colour I can't see. So I guess I can't trust myself to survive out there.

THERESE: In the big ugly world.

LEO: I don't think Karl has a girlfriend, you know.

THERESE: Leo. Sshh.

LEO: Bet he doesn't! Do you?

KARL: Not anymore.

LEO: How many wives have you had, Karl?

KARL: Not as many as you, mate. Just the one.

LEO: Did she steal all your money, destroy your manhood and then run off with some flash bastard in leather pants?

KARL: No.

LEO: Did she accuse you of philandering and selfishness and all manner of crimes you didn't commit?

KARL: No. She—uh—left when— Well, in the mess after the business went under, I must've been pretty hard to live with. She's with another guy now. About to have a baby.

LEO: So he's single. Available.

THERESE: Would you shut up! It's his private business. Anyway, I'm sure Karl can get some really nice woman if he decides—

KARL: Well, Karl's prob'ly not much use to anyone so—

THERESE: See? He doesn't want a girlfriend.

KARL: Oh, well... I—

There's a knock on the door.

THERESE: Great.

LEO: Who's that?

THERESE: Surprise for your birthday.

She opens the door to MARGO.

Hi. Thanks heaps for coming. Margo's come to say happy birthday.

MARGO *becomes aware of the decorations and presents.*

MARGO: Oh, I didn't realise it was going to be quite such a—uh... Happy birthday, Leo.

LEO *nods his acknowledgement warily.*

THERESE: Perfect timing. Dinner'll be ready soon and we can all go the fang.

MARGO: [*quietly to* THERESE] You should have told me the kind of thing you were— I didn't bring a present or—

THERESE: Thought you might not come if I made it sound like a big deal. And anyway, you being here today is the fantastic thing. Everybody siddown. I'll just—uh—

> THERESE *rushes off to get drinks.* MARGO *is surprised to see* KARL.

MARGO: Oh. Hello again.

KARL: Hello.

LEO: Karl's my friend. [*To* KARL] She doesn't think I have any friends.

THERESE: Leo. Give it a rest.

LEO: Did you clock her face when she walked in here? She couldn't believe it. [*To* MARGO] Yes! Yes! Good times with my friends!

THERESE: Who wants some punch? Non-alcoholic of course. Dinner and then birthday cake.

> *She serves everyone punch.*

This is nice, eh. All of us here like this.

LEO: This is marvellous! Like the old days! People dropping round for a drink!

KARL: Dinner smells fantastic.

THERESE: We're having one of Leo's favourites.

LEO: From my own recipe collection.

THERESE: [*to* MARGO] Oh—you probably ate stuff like this when you were a little kid in Greece. You were so lucky to get to live in Greece and Spain and all those other places. Was it really fantastic?

MARGO: Kids don't want to be dragged around the world because their father has a whim to paint in different light conditions. Kids want to stay in one place and go to the same set of swings every day.

> LEO *mutters and laughs to himself.* THERESE *shooshes him.*

KARL: Anyway, it smells fantastic, Therese.

MARGO: Yes. Delicious.

THERESE: I could never cook to save myself before. But then the other week, we found this envelope full of recipes and Leo's been teaching me to cook.

LEO *hoots a laugh.*

KARL: What?

THERESE: He isn't teaching me in the regular way. I do my best following the recipe on my own and if I get it wrong—

LEO *makes a retching noise and mimes spitting out the food.*

He spits the food out. Deadset.

LEO: Good incentive for her to get it right the next time.

THERESE: That's his teaching method. [*To* MARGO] Did Leo teach you to cook when you were a little kid?

MARGO: No.

LEO: When do I get my presents?

THERESE: Oh yeah, presents. I guess we can open them before we eat.

THERESE *fetches the parcels.*

KARL: Open mine first, Leo.

LEO *tears the paper off Karl's present. It's a letterbox made from pieces of New Guinea carved timber.*

LEO: Therese, we need a new letterbox, don't we!

KARL: I made it out of the bits of that smashed-up table.

LEO: Thank you, Karl. You always know exactly what I need. [*To* MARGO] Karl has the gift of kindness, you know.

THERESE: Well, he's always been very kind to us. It's beautiful. You're very clever, Karl.

LEO: What's this one?

LEO *grabs a rectangular parcel, prettily wrapped.*

THERESE: I don't know. It got brought by courier this morning.

THERESE *opens the attached note while* LEO *struggles to get the ribbons off like a greedy kid.*

LEO: [*boasting to* MARGO] You see? Old friends remembering my birthday. Dropping off presents. I still have a rich and full life, you know.

THERESE: It just says '*Ole*' on the front. Maybe someone sent it from Spain.

LEO: Could be. Barcelona. New York. Paris. I've got friends all over the world!

THERESE: 'Happy birthday, Leo. Best, Gavin.' Oh, Gavin… he's that guy who—

> LEO *unwraps a box with a bottle of tequila inside.* THERESE *quickly gets it off him.*

Well, it was nice of Gavin to think of you but this stuff's not the go for us anymore, eh.

> *She runs to put the bottle in the kitchen and points out the remaining parcel to distract him.*

Hey, you haven't opened my one.

> LEO *holds the large, square present.*

LEO: What is it?

THERESE: I couldn't spend up big on you, like I would've liked, so I—

From left: Andy Rodoreda as Karl, Kate Mulvany as Therese, Martin Vaughan as Leo and Victoria Longley as Margo in the 2004 Griffin Theatre production. (Photo: Robert McFarlane)

Well, open it.

LEO *opens it—it's a large album.*

I bought the album at the art gallery shop while you were busy ear-bashing some poor lady about Whiteley.

LEO: Sneaky.

THERESE: Then I went through those boxes of junk upstairs and fished out photos of the kids and holidays and special events. Check out—there's a section that shows this house being built. [*She leans across to flick to that part.*] You can see that wall going up. And the kids are little in some of the shots.

LEO *looks through the album.*

Do you like it?

KARL: It's wonderful.

MARGO: My God, I haven't seen any of these photos for years.

THERESE *is so driven and determinedly cheerful that she doesn't notice* LEO *has gone quiet, sombre.*

KARL: Who's that woman looking straight at the camera?

LEO: Phyllis.

THERESE: Leo's first wife. Margo's mum.

LEO: Phyllis. Look at her hair, her eyes. I completely forgot what she looked like.

THERESE: Don't panic. That's why I made the album. So you can see everyone and remember.

Overcome, LEO *loses his grip and the album starts to slide off his lap.* THERESE *catches it and flips to another page.*

Check out this cute one of little Henry. [*She leaps across the room to stand in a certain spot.*] He's standing right over here by this wall. See?

MARGO *and* KARL *lean over to look at the photo.*

Back then this wall was made of corrugated iron that Leo painted up.

MARGO: [*smiling*] Oh, yeah. I remember that.

LEO *shuffles towards the stairs.*

THERESE: Where are you off to?

LEO: Something I need to look for.

THERESE: Oh. Okay. But don't be long 'cos we're eating in a sec.

> LEO *goes off to the kitchen.*

Look at that shot—shows how far this ceiling has sagged since then, eh.

> MARGO *wanders around the room, leaving* KARL *going through the album on his own.*

MARGO: I don't know how you stand living in the house the way it is now.

THERESE: This house must've been a wild place to grow up.

MARGO: In some ways it was fun—for a little kid. I mean, you can't paint on the walls in a normal house.

THERESE: Not without getting a belting anyway. You kids used to paint on the walls?

MARGO: Mostly it was Leo. He'd be telling us a story and he'd suddenly grab a paintbrush and start illustrating it all over the bedroom wall.

THERESE: I bet he did, the naughty bugger.

MARGO: Leo could be a lot of fun when it suited him.

THERESE: Yeah? Like what?

MARGO: Oh, all sorts of things. One year he came back from a trip to New Guinea and we—me, my half-brother and Leo—we had a spear throwing contest against that wall.

THERESE: I always wondered what the little holes were. [*She glances over* KARL*'s shoulder and her attention is taken by one of the photos. To* MARGO] Is this you? It looks like you. How old would you be there? Four or five?

> MARGO *crosses back to look at the album.*

MARGO: Oh, my God… Ha! I was allowed to pick out that swimming costume for my sixth birthday.

THERESE: Yeah, you look pretty pleased with the whole 'I'm-in-this-sensational-pink-cossie' thing.

MARGO: [*laughing*] I certainly do.

THERESE: There's your mum.

KARL: Would Leo have taken that shot?

MARGO: Possibly. I think… Yes. He did take that one.

THERESE: What an excellent gummy smile.

MARGO: Listen, Therese, while Leo's not here, let me explain something to you—so you can explain to him.

THERESE: What?

> MARGO *picks up a brightly-coloured folder.*

MARGO: I've got some good news. I've been looking at Leo's financial situation—in the long-term—and I've come to an arrangement with the bank. We're going to raise a loan against the value of this land.

THERESE: But Leo could still live here?

MARGO: That's the idea. This way we maintain the house for the rest of his life plus generate cash for his living expenses. Enough to pay for a carer and whatever else he's likely to need.

THERESE: [*calling to the kitchen*] Leo! Margo's got some fantastic news! An excellent surprise! It's like another birthday present!

MARGO: Oh, I wouldn't put it like that.

THERESE: [*calling*] Come on! Quick!

> LEO *emerges from the kitchen, the tequila bottle stuffed in his vest. He's already quite drunk. He notices the official papers in* MARGO*'s hands.*

LEO: What's she got there? I won't sign anything.

THERESE: No, Leo, you don't understand. Let Margo explain. These are bank papers about the house. It's great. She's—

LEO: Therese, don't let her kick me out of my house.

THERESE: Calm down. She's not doing that.

MARGO: This means you won't have to leave the house.

THERESE: See? Margo's fixed it with the bank so you can keep the house no matter what. This is the best birthday present you could ever get.

LEO: Selling off my house on my birthday!

THERESE: No. That's not right. Listen—

LEO: I don't want tricks. She wants to sell my house. Can't you wait till I'm dead? She wants me dead.

MARGO *keeps her eyes down.*

THERESE: No. You don't understand. Just listen—

LEO: See? She doesn't even try to deny it. She wants me dead.

THERESE: Come on, Leo, don't do this.

> LEO *pulls the tequila out and takes a swig. The bottle is a third empty.*

What!? What are you—? Oh…

LEO: She's hovering over my rotting body, waiting for me to die.

MARGO: Look, I might go.

> MARGO *collects up the papers but* LEO *snatches them from her.*

LEO: Therese doesn't wish me dead like you do.

THERESE: Leo, give me the bottle.

> LEO *moves out of* THERESE'*s reach and drops the papers all over the floor.* MARGO *gathers them up.* LEO *rushes to her, sobbing.*

LEO: I'm your father. Your father. Was I so terrible? Is that why you can't love me? Was I such a vile creature to you?

THERESE: He's only saying these things because he's drunk. He doesn't mean—

MARGO: He means it. Booze doesn't change a person. It only loosens the tongue.

LEO: I'm not vile to Therese. Am I, Therese? You tell her. I'm good… I can be good.

THERESE: It'd be good if you gave me the bottle right now.

LEO: I did my best… why can't you love me? You pay a stranger to look after me.

THERESE: He's talking like this because he feels ashamed and he wants—

MARGO: You think? I think he's a self-pitying drunk wanting me to tell him lies.

LEO: Don't say cruel things to me. Therese, why is she saying…? Ohhh… Therese—a stranger—she cares more about me than my own daughter.

THERESE: Leo, stop. That's enough.

LEO: Therese loves me. Finally I know what a real loving child is like. Why can't you be my real loving child like Therese?

MARGO: Your 'real loving child' is only here because she's paid to be.

LEO: Therese loves me.

MARGO: Yeah? For all you know, she's just hanging around here to rip you off. It's not hard to take advantage of a friendless, dying, old dickhead.

LEO: You're a jealous bitch! You understand nothing about love!

LEO clutches the bottle to his belly and runs up the stairs. MARGO heads for the door. THERESE rushes to block her path.

THERESE: Please please, don't go off and think— It was my fault. I wanted everything to be— He's been getting so much better, remembering more. I know it can be better with you and him—

MARGO: Oh. You know.

THERESE: I know I pushed too fast and that's why he went off at the mouth but please don't go away thinking—

MARGO: What the fuck are you doing here? Who are you? Another one of the leeches trying to suck money out of him?

THERESE: What? No... please don't say—

MARGO: Make him dependent on you, ration his alcohol, sack the respite nurses to get total control. Is that what you're doing?

THERESE: Eh? No, the other nurses were upsetting—

MARGO: Straight-out stealing? Is that it? A thief pinching anything you can get your grubby hands on.

THERESE: No, no. That's not true.

MARGO: Given your history, I wouldn't be surprised.

THERESE: I haven't stolen anything.

MARGO: No, no. You're just very stupid. So stupid you thought a bit of robust family therapy would clear the air.

THERESE: I'm trying to look after him the best I can.

MARGO: And all you've managed to do is churn up the sludge at the bottom of the cess-pit.

THERESE: I was only wanting—

MARGO: Do you know how dangerous you are? Do you know what an almighty fucking mess you've created?

THERESE: I pushed too fast—

MARGO: I think you'd better shut up now.

KARL: Hey—I know it's not my business but—

MARGO: No, it's not your business. It's mine. In the end, it's me who gets stuck with cleaning up the mess. This isn't going to work anymore. Leo staying in this house. A parade of people like you turning up. I think the best thing is if I sort out some new arrangement. I want you to pack your things and be gone tomorrow morning.

THERESE: What? You want me to—?

MARGO: You can stay here tonight but you'll have to leave in the morning.

THERESE: I don't understand what you're—

MARGO: It's not complicated. You're sacked. I want you out of here.

MARGO *exits.* THERESE *is too stunned to speak for a moment.*

THERESE: I never ever thought about stealing from Leo.

KARL: I know that. You don't have to tell me that.

THERESE: I even know where there are drawings hidden in this house. Leo's told me. I could've stolen them but I didn't.

KARL: You're not that kind of person.

THERESE: She can just go, 'You're a thief', 'You're sacked'.

KARL: When Margo calms down, she'll change her mind.

THERESE: She won't. A person like her. The way she talked about me…

KARL: I can't believe she'd really sack you.

THERESE: You heard her! Believe it. Believe that people can be maggots, and idiots like me get shafted. That's how the world works, okay? Margo's right. I'm stupid. Thick. A retard.

KARL: Don't say that. It's not true.

THERESE: How many gullible idiots could they find to live in this dump and look after an old drunk?

KARL: I can't think of anyone who could do this job the way— You do an amazing job.

THERESE: But that doesn't fucking count.

KARL: Listen, listen, let me talk to Margo. When she calms down—

THERESE: Leo told me there are drawings hidden in the wall cavity right here. I could take them right now—easily.

KARL: I guess you could. But you're not like that.

THERESE: Margo thinks I am. 'Grubby hands'.

KARL: No, Margo doesn't think you're stealing. That's not what she said. She didn't say—

LEO *appears on the stairs. He's drunker and more spiteful.*

LEO: Stop that wretched noise. I can't sleep for all the noise. [*He staggers downstairs, holding the two-thirds empty bottle.*] Ah, I see you're entertaining your chippie boyfriend.

THERESE: Karl's not my boyfriend.

LEO: He's a dickless wonder.

THERESE: Don't say one more word. Go to bed.

LEO: I heard the shouting down here! Managed to get The Viper upset, didn't you? Now she's gonna sell my house from under me! Thanks to you, interfering bitch. [*He presses his fingers into his upper abdomen.*] Oh, I've got pain here.

THERESE: Because of the tequila you poured down your gullet.

LEO: Shut up. You're only here because The Viper pays you to wipe the arse of the old pisspot.

KARL: Leo, you don't want to talk to Therese like that. You don't really mean—

THERESE: Stay out of it, Karl.

LEO: [*to* KARL] Why did she come here? Couldn't get a job anywhere else? No. She enjoys feeling superior. Must be a rare treat for someone as low on the shit-pile as her. 'Oh, here's this pathetic old drunk. I can feel superior to him!'

THERESE: I never thought that.

LEO: But she was wrong! I have been someone important and she's just some lowlife slag.

KARL: Leo. Go upstairs and sleep it off.

LEO: She's just like all the others. She's a vulture picking on my carcass before I'm dead. 'Oh, Leo, you're gorgeous.' So I'll leave it all to her in my will. The beloved carer Therese inherits the Bailey estate.

THERESE: Shut up now, Leo. Please.

LEO: Oh, don't snivel.

KARL: Leo—stop. That's enough.

> KARL *tries to ease* LEO *away gently.* LEO *shakes him off.*

LEO: Who are you? Go away.

> LEO *circles* THERESE, *pressing his face close to her.*

Look at you. No wonder your poor bloody parents are ashamed of you. What scrap of joy did you ever bring to them? None. Their daughter's a thief and a slut and a liar. Ripping off the hairdresser lady. What an ugly little story that is. Your parents be better off never laying eyes on you again.

> THERESE *slaps* LEO *across the face repeatedly. She slaps him hard, out of control.* LEO *reels helplessly and collapses into a chair.* THERESE *is poised to hit him again when* KARL *restrains her.*

KARL: Therese. Stop. You don't want to do this.

> THERESE *backs away, gulps for breath.*

It's okay. You're okay, aren't you Leo? Therese, let's just all calm down.

THERESE: Look what I did.

KARL: But that wasn't you. You're not really like that.

THERESE: This is me. Use your eyes.

KARL: Let's all calm down. Leo looks okay.

THERESE: Shut up, Karl.

> THERESE *feels along the wall she indicated earlier.*

KARL: What are you doing?

THERESE: Finding the hiding spot.

> THERESE *hacks into the wall, tearing the woodwork apart.*

KARL: Oh no, Therese, stop. You're not this kind of person.

THERESE: I am. I've stolen stuff before. I've been in jail. This is the kind of person I am.

KARL: Not the person I've seen.

THERESE: Go away. Don't look at me.

KARL: Look, Leo's okay. He got a fright but you haven't really hurt him.

THERESE: I said go away.

THERESE *pulls a section loose to reveal the cavity.*

KARL: I can't believe you're doing this.

THERESE *pulls a package out of the cavity—two drawings wrapped in plastic.*

What are you going to do with those?

THERESE: Sell them. Get myself some money.

KARL: Come on, Therese.

THERESE *wraps the drawings in a rug.*

THERESE: Don't look at me. Fuck you. Don't look at me. Are you fucking deaf? I can feel your eyes on me. Fuck off.

KARL *flinches against the vicious tone in her voice but stands his ground.* THERESE *is acutely aware of him looking at her. Her manic energy suddenly flags. She drops the drawings on the ground and flops against the wall.*

KARL: Therese—

THERESE: I don't want you looking at me. Get out! Get out!

KARL *leaves.* THERESE *doesn't move and* LEO *is slumped in a stupor on the other side of the room as the house sinks into darkness.*

SCENE TWO

The next morning.

LEO *is asleep where he collapsed the night before. The drawings wrapped in the rug lie on the floor where* THERESE *dropped them. There's no sign of* THERESE.

MARGO *enters, carrying a couple of empty cardboard boxes. She sees the sleeping* LEO *and then notices the torn-apart wall. She unfolds the rug to find the drawings inside.*

LEO *mumbles as he wakes up, hung over.*

MARGO: Are you all right?

LEO: Where's Therese? Therese!

MARGO: I assume she's already gone. [*Indicating the wall and the drawings*] What happened here?

LEO: It wasn't me.

MARGO: Did she do this? Why are these drawings on the floor?

LEO: I don't know. I don't feel well.

MARGO: Hungover. That's why.

> LEO *curls up, muttering miserably.* THERESE *appears at the top of the stairs, carrying the sportsbags she arrived with.*

I thought you'd already left.

THERESE: I was waiting for an agency nurse to get here.

MARGO: We're moving him into a nursing home today.

THERESE: Oh…

LEO: What? What did she say? Did she say nursing home?

MARGO: He needs professional care.

LEO: [*to* THERESE] You can't let her do this to me.

MARGO: I'll be here packing his clothes. So you can go.

> THERESE *nods. She collects up her belongings and shoves them in the sportsbags.* MARGO *packs some of Leo's things into a cardboard box.* LEO *gets more agitated as his head clears. He follows* THERESE *around the room.*

LEO: Therese, don't leave me. Is it because I said terrible things to you last night?

THERESE: It's not that. I have to go.

LEO: Don't go. Please. I need you. Don't let them pack me off to a home.

> MARGO *has a proper look at the drawings wrapped in the rug.*

MARGO: [*to* THERESE] What's going on with these drawings?

> THERESE *stays silent, eyes down.*

LEO: [*to* THERESE] Say you'll stay. Say you'll forgive me.

MARGO: You're asking her to forgive you? What do you think she was going to do with these?

> MARGO *shows him the drawings.*

LEO: I don't care.

MARGO: It looks like she was going to steal from you, doesn't it?

LEO: But she didn't take them, did she. Therese. Please. Please stay and help me.

THERESE: You'll be better off in a place where they can look after you.

LEO: Are you leaving me because of things I said?

THERESE: No. Margo's right. I was going to steal from you. And I hurt you.

LEO: [*to* MARGO] She didn't hit me hard.

MARGO: You hit him?

THERESE: Yes. I slapped him.

LEO: Not very hard. Not very hard. I deserved it. Therese was right to slap me and look, look, look—I'm all right now. So don't worry about that. Therese, stay and look after me.

THERESE: Leo, I hit you and that's— I can't look after you, okay? I have to go.

MARGO: Yes. I'd like you to leave now. [*To* LEO] I'm going to pack your clothes, okay? Let's not get any more upset. Let's do what needs to be done.

> MARGO *picks up the drawings and takes them upstairs with her.* THERESE *grabs her bags and heads for the door.* LEO *rushes to block her path.*

LEO: Wait. Wait. I can't leave here yet. There are paintings in this house. Precious paintings.

THERESE: Margo will take care of them.

LEO: No, no. Not the ones you can see. Ones I've hidden. You've got to stay and help me find them before they ship me off to a home.

THERESE: I can't. You should tell Margo—

LEO: You're leaving because of the cruel things I said.

THERESE: No. I told you—

> LEO *starts whacking at his own mouth with his hand.*

LEO: I'll take the words back. I wish I could stop them coming out of mouth.

THERESE *grabs his hand to stop him hurting himself.*

You look after me. I need you.

THERESE: There'll be proper people to look after you.

LEO: No. You. I want you.

THERESE: I'm no good to you. I'm an awful person, okay Leo? That's the truth.

LEO: No, you're not.

THERESE: An awful, ugly person.

LEO: No, no. Wait! I can show you. I can show you—wait, wait.

He grips THERESE*'s arm. Then he runs to a hiding spot and pulls out the piece of fibro he drew on in Act One. He hands the drawing to* THERESE. *She falls silent.*

I watched you when you couldn't see me. I drew you. See? See? It's you! It's your beauty.

He watches anxiously as THERESE *stares at the drawing.*

I can't draw as well as— My bloody hand shakes. I was going to wait, make it better.

THERESE: This is beautiful.

LEO: It's you!

He watches her face carefully as she looks at the drawing.

Yes. Yes. Good. You can see.

MARGO *comes back downstairs with packed boxes.*

MARGO: Your friend—that builder—he's outside in his truck.

THERESE *is so transfixed by the drawing that she doesn't register this.*

LEO: Karl? Karl is out there? [*He runs just outside the door, yelling out.*] Karl! Karl! Come in!

THERESE *sits down, staring at the drawing.* MARGO *moves around the room, packing items into the boxes.*

[*Shouting to* KARL] Hurry! Help me look for the precious paintings.

KARL *appears at the door, tentative.* LEO *drags him inside.*

Talk to Therese. Make her stay and help me.

THERESE: What are you doing back here?

KARL: Well, I never went away. Been sitting outside in my truck all night.

MARGO: So what do you want?

KARL: I'm a friend of Leo and Therese. I wanted to make sure everything was okay.

LEO *rushes up to clutch at* KARL.

LEO: Make Therese stay and help me.

MARGO: [*to* THERESE] Leo's getting distressed again. You're not helping the situation by being here.

LEO: There are paintings hidden in the house! If the house is demolished, they'll be destroyed!

MARGO: Will you leave now please?

KARL: Can't Leo look for the pictures?

MARGO: If there are any hidden paintings, they'll be found.

KARL: That might be right, but can't Leo—?

MARGO: [*to* LEO] Come on, get your things and we'll go.

MARGO *pulls shoes out of the cardboard box.*

LEO: No. No.

KARL: He has the right to stay in his house until he's ready.

MARGO: There's no one to look after him and he can't be left here alone.

THERESE *is tentative at first:*

THERESE: Well… I could look after him.

LEO: Please.

MARGO: You've been sacked if you remember.

THERESE: I could—I mean, I could stay on anyway if Leo wants me to.

MARGO: What? Someone who's been physically abusive towards a sick old man. You're not fit to look after him.

LEO: I'm all right. I want Therese.

MARGO: I could have a medical assessment done that'd get Leo scheduled.

THERESE: Well, you could do that, yeah…

MARGO: I will if I have to.

THERESE: But until then, I guess I'll stay here… as long as Leo needs to.

LEO: Yes. Yes.

MARGO: There is no way she can stay here.

LEO: It's still my house. If I say Therese can stay, she can stay.

MARGO: She's not your carer anymore, Leo. She's a thief who's been sacked.

THERESE: I'd just be here as Leo's friend.

MARGO: If you insist on interfering with proper care, decided by the family, I'll have to ring the police.

LEO: Police—ha. It's not trespassing if I invite her.

MARGO: I'm not talking about trespass. I'm talking about malicious damage and assault. [*To* THERESE] I know you're on a suspended sentence at the moment. If you don't leave now, I will press charges. That'll mean going back to jail, won't it?

> THERESE *nods.* LEO *looks nervously at her.*

THERESE: Well, I guess—

MARGO: You better just go.

THERESE: Well, I guess that's up to you. Me and Leo are going to stay and look for the stuff he thinks is here.

> LEO *whoops with delight.*

LEO: Upstairs! Help me look in the back room upstairs.

> LEO *runs towards the stairs, wanting* THERESE *to follow.*

THERESE: Yeah… just give me a minute.

KARL: I'll help you, mate.

> KARL *follows* LEO *up the stairs.* THERESE *carefully carries the drawing of herself and puts it in one of her sportsbags. Then she starts to clean up the debris from the damaged wall.*

MARGO: Why are you taking this risk? Do you think I won't really ring the police?

THERESE: I guess you will. I don't know. I'm just making this up as I go.

MARGO: What's this big sacrifice for? To help a nasty, selfish old drunk stay in his house for a few days? Why does he deserve it? Don't you know who that man is?

THERESE: I think I know.

MARGO: He doesn't deserve your devotion.

THERESE: If all of us only got what we deserved, most of us'd be pretty fucked.

MARGO: There's got to be some fairness. Someone who's lived the life he's lived—why should he get away with it?

THERESE: It's not up to me to judge him like that. I think maybe you have a right to but—

MARGO: You love his paintings? You think they absolve him of every foul thing he's done?

THERESE: No. But you can't count the foul things harder against him because he painted those.

MARGO: I want to see the honest balance sheet on Leo Bailey. That's what I want to see.

THERESE: He made some beautiful things. Don't they count on the balance sheet too?

MARGO: When I look at them, I don't see beautiful. I see the life of all the women he married and the children he spawned—I see the marrow he sucked out of them and spewed out onto the canvas.

THERESE: He's started to see some of that too and he's ashamed.

MARGO: He should feel ashamed. He's got plenty to be ashamed about.

LEO *appears on the stairs, unseen by* MARGO *and* THERESE.

That man said so many cruel things to me—when I was eleven years old—I remember the words exactly—'What scrap of joy have you ever brought anyone? Not your poor bloody mother. Not me.'

THERESE: He never meant half those things. He was drunk or—

MARGO: That makes it worse. Cruel without even caring. Dumping his ugly moods on a little kid. Saying things he wouldn't even remember an hour later.

LEO *whimpers, unheard by* MARGO *and* THERESE.

I saw him slice into my mother over and over. She put up with it. When he finally turned his back on her—that's what tore her apart. She lay in bed in the dark for a year before she killed herself.

LEO: Oh, my Phyllis…

MARGO: Leo Bailey is like a sac of poison in my belly. Toxins leak out into my system if I'm not vigilant. Whatever you think of me—

THERESE: If I was you, I'd feel the same way.

Too distressed to speak, MARGO *leaves.* THERESE *hears* LEO *murmuring on the stairs.*

LEO: My Phyllis... my girl...

THERESE: Leo, it's okay.

LEO: It's not. It's not. Don't tell me lies.

He stumbles down the stairs. KARL *follows him down, trying to steady him.*

It's too late.

THERESE: It's not too late. You can talk to Margo.

LEO: No. It's too late. I can feel my body crumbling apart from the inside.

He falls. THERESE *and* KARL *go to help him up but* LEO *stays there, staring at the floor.*

The floor. The painting is hidden in the floor.

KARL: Under the floorboards?

LEO: We have to find it.

THERESE: How do we—?

KARL: I'll get the tools from the truck.

*KARL *runs outside.*

LEO: I remember. That's where it is. We have to find it. We have to find it now.

THERESE: Calm down. We will.

*LEO *paces, muttering to himself.*

Which part of the floor?

LEO: I'm trying to remember.

He shakes his head, searching, muttering. He yanks at rotten floorboards with all his strength.

Where is it? Try here.

THERESE: Don't hurt yourself. We'll help you.

LEO: Oh—maybe under that window.

*THERESE *works to lift a floorboard. In places the boards are* *so loose that even* LEO *can lift them by hand. He becomes more and more frantic.*

THERESE: What are we looking for?

LEO: A tube. It's in a metal tube.

THERESE: Take it easy, Leo. We'll find it. Don't get yourself in a state.

LEO: You don't understand.

THERESE: I understand you want to find a painting and we'll keep—

LEO: No. No. It's not 'a' painting. It's the only one I care about.

THERESE: 'The Laughing Girl'? I thought that was missing.

LEO: They all thought so.

> KARL *re-enters with tools. He uses a pinch bar to lift up a floor-board.*

THERESE: But really you hid it?

LEO: Years ago. We must find it.

THERESE: We will. Calm down.

KARL: [*to* THERESE] Do you think it's here? He might just—

THERESE: He might just want it to be here.

LEO: Stop whispering about me. I can hear you.

KARL: Are you sure you hid it in this house?

LEO: Yes. Yes. I completely forgot I hid it. Thought they'd stolen it. But now I remember. Here! Here! Quickly!

> KARL *yanks up boards where* LEO *is pointing.*

I didn't want them bickering about it—like scrawny mongrels fighting over a carcass. [*He feels around under the floor.*] I knew they'd try to steal it and then wait for me to die. Couldn't let that happen with this one. Ah! There she is.

> *He pulls out a stainless steel tube.*

THERESE: Is that it? Is that the one?

> LEO *is too weak to yank the top off the tube.*

I'll do it.

LEO: Be careful!

> THERESE *pulls out a rolled canvas and hands it to* LEO. *The three of them huddle round as* LEO *unrolls the canvas. We*

Kate Mulvany as Therese, Martin Vaughan as Leo and Andy Rodoreda (behind) as Karl in the 2004 Griffin Theatre production. (Photo: Robert McFarlane)

can't see the picture itself. LEO's *face lights up.* THERESE *and* KARL *are transfixed by it.*

THERESE: My God… Oh, Leo, it's so lovely.

LEO: Isn't she?

KARL: She's beautiful. How long ago did you paint it?

LEO: Oh, years. Years and years. Before everything went wrong.

THERESE: Oh, look at her. She's shining out at us.

KARL: How old is the little girl?

LEO: Six. She was six. Radiant girl.

KARL: You can practically hear her laughing.

THERESE: Yes!

LEO: When she laughed—oh… the most delicious laugh… intoxicating. It filled me up. I loved hearing my girl laugh. Precious girl.

KARL: The girl in the picture—who is she?

LEO: Why wouldn't she be laughing? Everything was good then.

THERESE: It's Margo.

LEO: Yes. It's her.

> *He starts to cry. He walks away, leaving* KARL *and* THERESE *holding the canvas.*

I couldn't hold her in my head long enough. I let myself forget how luminous she was. Went off chasing other things. Stupid vanity, flimsy thrills, some gratification, some itch! Look at the precious things I had. Look what I've done. Look what I've done.

THERESE: Leo—

LEO: It's more than I can bear.

> LEO *is swaying, woozy.*

KARL: Has Margo ever seen this painting?

LEO: Oh… I don't know. Years ago maybe…

THERESE: Why don't you show the—? No, why don't you give the painting to Margo?

LEO: If I give it to her, do you think she'll forgive me? I'll give her the painting and she'll forgive me!

THERESE: No, I don't think… you can't expect that.

LEO: You're right…

THERESE: But Leo—
LEO: One painting can't fix everything.
THERESE: No.
LEO: It's not enough.
THERESE: It's not.

> LEO *moans.*

But that doesn't mean you shouldn't give her the painting.
LEO: Do you think I should do that?
THERESE: Just give it to her.
LEO: Yes. Yes.

> KARL *notices that* LEO *is swaying, about to topple over.*

KARL: Whoa—watch out, mate.
LEO: I feel dizzy.
THERESE: Go upstairs and have a lie down.
LEO: Roll up the painting carefully.

> THERESE *carefully rolls up the canvas.*

KARL: Let me help you up.

> LEO *waves him away and starts up the stairs.*

LEO: I'm right. Just need a lie down. We'll give her the painting.
THERESE: Yes.

> LEO *disappears upstairs.* THERESE *puts the painting back in the tube. She's shaky, overcome.*

KARL: You right there?

> *He reaches to steady her. She pulls away.*

Why is it so terrible—me being nice to you?
THERESE: Oh… I don't mean to—
KARL: Makes me feel like a bit of a soft fool.
THERESE: Oh no, don't. It's me. I'm not used to the feel of it. It's strange, like clothes that don't fit.
KARL: I don't understand that.

> THERESE *won't keep still, throwing herself into straightening up the floorboards.* KARL *watches her.*

THERESE: What are you looking at? Don't look at me.

KARL: Keep still. Let me look at you.

THERESE: What?

> *She freezes.* KARL *comes closer and slowly leans forward.*
> *They kiss—cautious but tender.*

You don't want me.

KARL: I do.

THERESE: You don't. You don't know what kind of person I am.

KARL: I know what— Oh, I'm not going to argue with you about it. I just— Oh... I'm not good at this.

THERESE: Me neither.

> *They smile.*

KARL: Can I at least look at you?

> THERESE *stays still and lets him look. Eventually she meets his gaze and smiles. There's a cry from* LEO.

THERESE: Leo? You okay?

LEO: I'm being sick. I'm...

THERESE: I'm coming.

> LEO *appears on the stairs, blood all down his shirt.*

LEO: There's blood.

THERESE: Oh, Leo...

> *She and* KARL *help him down the rest of the stairs.*

Feel like you might be sick again?

LEO: No. No. I feel better now.

THERESE: Good. Sit down here. I'll clean you up.

> *They sit* LEO *in an armchair.* THERESE *hurries to get a bowl of water and whispers to* KARL.

We need an ambulance.

KARL: You'll be right, Leo. Therese'll look after you. [*To* THERESE] They'll have trouble finding this place. I'll wait out there, direct them—if you're okay to—

THERESE: Yeah. Do that. Tell them I think it's an upper G.I. bleed.

KARL *hurries out, dialling triple-o in his mobile.* THERESE *loosens* LEO*'s bloody shirt.*

Let's get this mucky thing off you.

She crouches close to him and sponges the blood off his neck and chest.

Is the water too cold?

LEO: No. It feels good.

THERESE: What a mess, eh. Karl's ringing the ambulance. You'll be right. It looks like a lot of blood but really—

LEO: No. Don't lie. I would like to know what's happening.

THERESE: I'm not a doctor or a nurse.

LEO: You read things, you talked to the doctors about things. Tell me.

THERESE: I think you're having a big bleed inside.

LEO: In my guts.

THERESE: Yes.

LEO: Feel my belly. [*He puts her hands on his belly.*] It's all swollen up.

THERESE: Because it's filling with blood.

LEO: Ha—but there's no pain.

THERESE: That's good.

LEO: But I'm dying. I think so.

THERESE *can't say anything.*

You won't leave me, will you?

THERESE: No, I'll stay right here.

LEO: I feel woozy—like I'm drunk. But I'm not.

THERESE *keeps sponging his face and neck.*

That feels good. Mmm... feels like my body is fading away. That's not so bad then, is it? Not so frightening.

THERESE: No.

LEO: Therese?

THERESE: I'm here.

LEO: Make sure you give the painting to her.

THERESE: I will.

LEO: You bring me a lot of joy, you know.

THERESE: Mmm.

LEO: Say you know.

THERESE: I know.

LEO: Ohh… feels like I'm sinking…

THERESE: I got you.

> LEO *fades into unconsciousness.* THERESE *holds him and keeps sponging his face. The sound of an ambulance siren.*

◆ ◆ ◆ ◆ ◆

SCENE THREE

Daytime. MARGO *is in the house, packing things into cardboard boxes and a packing crate.*

THERESE *enters.*

THERESE: Oh. Hello. Couple of things I needed to come back for. I'll be out of here in a sec.

MARGO: Fine. The funeral will probably be the middle of next week.

THERESE: Okay.

> MARGO *sits.*

MARGO: I always thought I'd feel released when he died. But I don't.

> THERESE *sits down nearby.*

I have a pretty accurate picture of how the pathology of this family works in my life. Doesn't fix it. Insight is overrated in my opinion.

> THERESE *fetches the metal tube with the painting in it.*

THERESE: We found this yesterday.

MARGO: Under the floorboards, I assume.

THERESE: It's 'The Laughing Girl'. Leo hid it.

MARGO: Ah.

THERESE: He really wanted me to give it to you.

MARGO: Sure. It'll go in with all the other—

THERESE: No. No, he wanted to give it to you personally.

MARGO: Oh.

THERESE *hands* MARGO *the tube.*

THERESE: Did you know it's you in the painting? The little girl?

MARGO: Oh… I suppose I did… I'm not sure.

THERESE: Well, it is you and Leo was— The thing is, he talked about you—when you were little. How lovely you were and how much— Luminous, he said. Precious girl. And he talked about how he wrecked everything— I'm not explaining this properly. He said—

MARGO: Don't bother. I don't want to hear it.

THERESE: Oh, but you should because—

MARGO: Why should I listen to his last big speech to you? He didn't say any of that to me. One painting doesn't make up for anything. So typical of Leo: to think some artistic gesture could do the job—easy— instead of proper human decency.

THERESE: I can understand why you think that and that's—that's fair enough.

MARGO *puts the tube on top of a packing crate.*

MARGO: It goes in the estate with the rest.

THERESE: Well, he really wanted you to have it.

MARGO *nods.*

I might see you at the funeral.

THERESE *finds her sportsbag and checks that Leo's drawing of her on the fibro is inside. She takes a moment to look at it, to enjoy it. Then she carefully packs the drawing in the bag and exits.*

MARGO *continues packing stuff into the cardboard box for a moment and then puts it down. She picks the metal tube out of the packing crate.*

She takes out the canvas and slowly unrolls it. She looks at the painting, transfixed by it.

THE END

*Victoria Longley as Margo in the 2004 Griffin Theatre production.
(Photo: Robert McFarlane)*

ALSO BY DEBRA OSWALD

Dags
Gilliam is 16, suffers from the occasional 'ack-attack' and is worried about not having a boyfriend. She loves chocolate and gelato, and is infatuated with the best-looking boy in school. *Dags* is a funny and compassionate look at the trials of adolescence: pimples, heartache and self-discovery.
ISBN 0 86819 180 9

Gary's House
Gary has failed in everything he has attempted. But when he inherits a block of land, he gets an urge to build a nest with Sue-Ann, his angry and pregnant girlfriend. *Gary's House* is a story about Aussie battlers—battling with each other, the elements and the world in their quest to turn a dream into reality. What begins as satire becomes a moving drama told with humour compassion and loving detail by a highly original and insightful playwright.
ISBN 0 86819 607 X

Skate
Any plans for a skate park in Narragindi are dead in the water. The kids of the town are left to skate on the town hall steps and take their chances avoiding the local police. Zac, a young leader among the many youth committees set up to get a skate park, wants no part of another attempt. His best mate, Corey, a guy with a troubled history, has a passion for the new campaign, sparked by his interest in Lauren, a member of the new committee. When tragedy strikes, the town is galvanised into action and what was originally a fight for a skate park grows into a struggle for acceptance and unity. *Skate* is a turbo-charged, moving and funny account of the mates, mothers, tricks and traumas of a group of young skaters. Enhanced by live skateboarding, the play is full of the emotional awkwardness of adolescence, its adrenalin, compassion and humour, and reflects the hopes and aspirations of young people in regional Australia.
ISBN 0 86819 727 0

Sweet Road
Jo is on the road. So too are Carla, Andy, Blake, Nicole and Browndog. Along with Yasmin, Michael, Frank and Curtis, each has a plan on where they are going and a determination to get there. But as their lives interweave and disperse and plans go awry, each of them discovers that the road they are travelling may not always take them where they expected, and if they are lucky, the destination may be more wonderful than any of them could ever have dreamed. Full of vitality and good humour, *Sweet Road* is a play which explores the aspirations and idiosyncrasies of seemingly ordinary people as they cross the vast and far from ordinary Australian landscape.
ISBN 0 86819 616 9

GRIFFIN THEATRE PRODUCTIONS AVAILABLE FROM CURRENCY PRESS

Reg Cribb
The Return
It's late, it's stifling hot and a commuter train travels from Perth to Fremantle. In the claustrophobic compartment two young men, recently out of prison, appear to have the upper hand. But all is not as it seems. As the distinction between aggressor and victim becomes increasingly ambiguous, the late-night journey rides an uneasy line between comedy and psychological thriller.
ISBN 0 86819 692 4

Michael Gurr
Julia 3
Julia is the enigmatic and elegant widow of an international financier. In her role as benefactor of a foundation established by her husband, she has the power to choose who shall benefit financially from his generosity. Among her chosen are a detective of art forgery, a medical scientist and a writer. But on what grounds were they selected and why exactly has she invited these three to her husband's funeral?
ISBN 0 86819 737 8

Katherine Thomson
Wonderlands
In 1931, Alice, a white station owner, goes riding with her Aboriginal head stockman and friend, Jim. During the course of the afternoon, they come to an agreement about the running of the property, Ambertrue, and its ownership. Many years later, in an environment of white paranoia fed by misinformation, Alice's great nephew Lon is running Ambertrue. When Lon receives a letter announcing a native title claim in the area, he is terrified that his dream of passing the family property on to his son-in-law will be shattered.
ISBN 0 86819 728 9

Ian Wilding
Torrez
Torrez knows how to kick a football. But at thirty-something he's on the wrong side of his playing career. His frazzled manager Foxy believes a media career beckons, but there may be one too many skeletons in the Torrez closet to get this sporting legend on primetime in the way they'd like. And then there's the terrible possibility that one of the skeletons is out of the closet and waiting at the front door for an autograph. *Torrez* is a raucously funny exposé of the world of celebrity and the longings at the heart of Australian masculinity, featuring two of the worst-behaved men seen on the Australian stage for a long time.
ISBN 0 86819 734 3

NEW TITLES FROM CURRENCY PRESS

Raimondo Cortese
Roulette
Edgy, provocative, and emotionally honest: each of the twelve plays of the *Roulette* series explores the nuances and subtleties that come into being when two people meet. From a chance meeting between a man and a woman in a café to the aggression of the prodigal son returning home to enslave a helpless older man, Cortese's fiercely intelligent writing illuminates the moments of cruelty or beauty that are inherent in any encounter between two people.
ISBN 0 86819 765 3

Michael Futcher and Helen Howard
The Drowning Bride
'Tell him I love him. Tell him I forgive him.' Her grandmother's last words send Ellen Burton, a young Brisbane artist, far out on a rip-tide of grief and guilt—anchor-less, unable to paint—to America and the Latvian grandfather she's never met. After the stories she has heard of his behaviour in Nazi-occupied Latvia, she expects to hate him. But in Grandad Valdis there is a seductive amalgam of charisma and cruelty which blurs the border of hate and love for Ellen. Grandma is dead. Which of them is to blame? Matt, the man Ellen wants to marry, watches their confrontation in anguish as his future flows from his grasp. Zenta, Valdis' great-niece—sexy, desperate, with nothing to lose—picks over the spoils of their battle. From the writers of the award-winning *A Beautiful Life*, Michael Futcher and Helen Howard's *The Drowning Bride* is an intimate drama laced with black humour, which will touch anyone who has ever known love, and betrayal, and the struggle to forgive.
ISBN 0 86819 773 4

Joanna Murray-Smith
Bombshells
When *Bombshells* premiered in Melbourne, the *Age* predicted that it would end up in London's West End: 'Get in quick if you want to be able to boast you were there where it all began', it advised readers. It was right. After an award-winning season in Edinburgh, *Bombshells* opened in London in September 2004. *Bombshells* exposes six women balancing their inner and outer lives with humour and often desperate cunning. They range in age from a feisty teenager to a 64-year-old widow yearning for the unexpected. Joanna Murray-Smith created these six dazzling monologues to showcase the talents of Caroline O'Connor, but they will be relished by performers everywhere.
ISBN 0 86819 751 3

For a full list of our titles, visit our website:

www.currency.com.au

Currency Press
The performing arts publisher
PO Box 2287
Strawberry Hills NSW 2012
Australia
enquiries@currency.com.au
Tel: (02) 9319 5877
Fax: (02) 9319 3649